Blue Venom

and

Forbidden Incense

THE LIBRARY OF BANGLADESH

SYED SHAMSUL HAQ

Blue Venom and *Forbidden Incense*

Two Novellas

TRANSLATED BY SAUGATA GHOSH

CALCUTTA LONDON NEW YORK

Seagull Books, 2018

ISBN 978 0 8574 2 501 0

The Library of Bangladesh series was conceived by the Dhaka Translation Center at the University of Liberal Arts Bangladesh. Find out more at http://dtc.ulab.edu.bd/

Printed in arrangement with Bengal Lights Books

This edition is not for sale in Bangladesh

British Library Cataloguing-in-Publication Data

A catalogue record for this book is available from the British Library

Typeset and designed by Sunandini Banerjee, Seagull Books, using artwork by Narottama Dobey and W. Basher from the Bengal Lights editions

Printed and bound by Maple Press, York, Pennsylvania, USA

LIBRARY OF BANGLADESH

An Introduction

The independence of Bangladesh, while into its fifth decade now, is still viewed by many outsiders as an accident of history. All historical outcomes are in part an accident, but any event of the magnitude of Bangladesh's liberation can only happen as a consequence of deep and long-term agency. What underlies that agency in this case most decisively is a unique cultural identity.

Like the soft deposits flowing down from the Himalayas that created the land mass known as Bangladesh today, its culture too has resulted from centuries of diverse overlay. Generations here have always gravitated towards the mystical branch of the reigning faith, be it Buddhism, Hinduism or Islam. The net effect is a culture that has always valued tolerance and detachment over harsh rituals or acquisitive fierceness.

There is no way better than Bangladesh's literature to know what makes this unique and vital culture as full as it is of glory and, of course, foibles. How did a rain-washed delta full of penniless peasants turn into a leader among developing nations? How did the soft, mystical, Baul-singing population turn into one of the fiercest guerilla armies of the last century? How did love of the Bangla language trigger the very march to freedom? How do the citizens of the world's most densely populated city, barring only a few tax or gambling enclaves, make sense of daily life, and find any beauty, amid all the breathless din of commerce and endless jostle of traffic?

The first three books in this series provide a remarkable window into the realities and mindscape of this amazing, confounding, rich world through translations of three of the living legends of Bangladeshi writing: Syed Shamsul Haq, Hasan Azizul Huq and Syed Manzoorul Islam. The presentation of their work has been made possible by the Dhaka Translation Center, hosted by the University of Liberal Arts Bangladesh. It also owes a great deal to the tireless efforts of its Director, Kaiser Haq. The series owes most, however, to award-winning translator Arunava Sinha, who both helped conceive of this idea, and helms it as series editor. Eminent translators brought together by him have ensured a rare and truly world-class rendition of these hidden gems of world literature. The impressive international-standard production owes everything to DTC's sister concern, Bengal Lights, led by editor Khademul Islam and managing editor, QP Alam.

Bangladesh, for all its success, is still to the world the sum of half-told stories told by others. It's high time to offer a fuller account of ourselves to the world. DTC plans to bring out at least three titles each year, and add both new names and new titles by selected authors to this defining series on Bangladeshi writing. We also believe that the process of consciously engaging new and wider audiences will lead to new refinements to a body of work that is already one of the great overlooked treasures of global writing.

KAZI ANIS AHMED

Publisher, Bengal Lights Books

Founder, Dhaka Translation Center

Blue Venom

1

Brown light fills the room all day. And all night. The windows, covered with brown paper, shut off the view outside. A naked bulb hangs overhead. Often, one can hear the sound of heavy footsteps, of one man or maybe two, in the corridor outside. Sometimes a motorcar is also heard, farther away.

He sits alone on the blanket-covered bed all day. He continues to sit the same way when night comes but sleep eludes him. At some point sleep comes to him naturally, and he drops off before being rudely woken up by a sharp prod. He opens his eyes and at first can only see the khaki uniform, close to his face. As his eyes clear he can see the unfamiliar features of the man in uniform.

He has not seen this soldier before. Must be new on the job.

"Get up."

He gets up and follows the soldier outside in silence. Once outside, the soldier pushes him ahead, following him but also monitoring his movements. Soon the two of them come to stand before a row of doors, one of which he is pushed through. Unlike the cell he was in, the toilet he is in now is neat and clean, with a washbasin. The floor is spotless and there is no stench in the air.

He blinks and looks at himself in the mirror above the washbasin. For a moment he mistakes his own reflection for that of someone else. He stands transfixed before the mirror, till the illusion passes and he can recognize himself again. He thinks he looks the same as before and for a moment he finds it easy to believe that he is standing in front of the mirror in his own house for a shave. He notices that his face is covered with a dark stubble.

It is now that he discovers a new smell that lingers on his clothes— the smell of gunpowder. For the last two days a one-sided battle had raged across the city with bullets flying, shells exploding, the air turning warm and pungent. The smell of that battle on his clothes now makes him feel nauseated. He still has no idea why he has been imprisoned here.

The soldier guarding him gives him another prod when he comes out and begins to follow him as before, as he walks on till they come before a second door. Another soldier, who stands guard before the door, now takes over and ushers him into a different room. He finds himself face to face with three officers seated across a pair of tables joined side to side. The tables are the color of glue from the *gaab* tree, empty, bereft of paper, pen or other objects. He cannot remember when he last saw anything as starched and well-ironed as the uniforms the officers wear, though the employees of the mercantile firm he used to work in were always encouraged by the boss to dress smartly. The collars, epaulettes and buttons appear to gleam in the light inside the room, as if they had all been carefully polished with wax.

The soldier who had escorted him nudges him and tells him to give the officers a salute. He hurriedly raises his hand in an exaggerated salute to pay his respects adequately. There is no response from anybody on the other side of the table, which he interprets as a response of sorts. The officers wear a look of quiet efficiency which assures him to some extent that he will now be released soon and be on his way to Jafarganj once again, just as he had been before he was captured.

Only the day before, like many others, he too had been stopped and searched by soldiers near Mirpur Bridge. But unlike the others, instead of being allowed to proceed after the inspection, he had been arrested and brought to this prison.

Shortly, one of the officers opens a cupboard and brings out a file. A red pencil appears in his hand miraculously without help from anyone else. At the same time another man comes in through a door on the other side, carrying a notebook and pencil and sits down at a small table nearby, the pencil poised in an expectant slant over an open page of the notebook.

Finally one of the officers beams at him sunnily and inquires politely if he has had a good night's rest. "Yes," he replies. Even though he has stayed up most of the night he does not find it appropriate to tell them that now. "I slept well," he tells them. "Good, good," the officer nods and says.

The second officer now lightens up and smiles at him. "We are not yet able to bring bedbugs and mosquitoes under our control and curtail their activities," he says. "We apologize for any inconvenience caused on that account. Sincerely."

He is touched by their concern, indeed overcome by it. The third officer cuts in after the second and asks if he has been served food or not. Though he has not eaten anything, given the easy bonhomie established between him and the officers, it appears unseemly to rat on their subordinates to them. So he remains quiet.

"Do you mean they haven't given you anything to eat?"

Immediately one of the officers summons a soldier who comes and stands at attention before them while the three pester him with questions. "Go and get food," one of them finally tells the soldier, "and get a chair too. Why do I have to remind you people that a visitor deserves a place to sit at?"

Miraculously, a chair appears in a moment. He sit down awkwardly, feeling uncomfortable. Even when he tries to change his posture, the discomfiture does not go away. When the interrogation begins he soon loses track of who is asking him what.

"Name?"

"Nazrul Islam."

"Kazi Nazrul Islam?"

"Yes, Kazi Nazrul Islam." He notices, from the corner of his eye, the pencil in the hand of the man with the notebook moving rapidly.

"Father's name?"

"Kazi Saiful Islam."

"Age?"

"Whose age? My father has passed away."

"Your age?"

"Forty-two."

"Place of birth?"

Nazrul hesitates.

"What is your place of birth?"

"Burdwan district."

"In India?"

"Yes, in West Bengal, India. We migrated to Dacca in 1948."

"And when did you start writing poetry?"

"Poetry?" Nazrul fails to comprehend the question and stares at each of them by turn. All three stare back at him, waiting for a reply.

Finally one of them shuffles in his seat, blinks once or twice and asks him for his address.

"My address?"

"Yes, where do you live in Dacca?"

"No 1, Gobindo Datta Lane, Laxmibazar. Very close to Sadarghat."

"Isn't Gobindo Datta a Hindu name?"

"*Ji*, it is a Hindu name."

"You are Hindu."

"No, I am not."

"Muslim?"

"Yes, I am Muslim."

"Was your father Muslim?"

"I have told you, his name was Kazi Saiful Islam. He was Muslim."

"Shia or Sunni?"

"Sunni, not Shia."

"How many books of poetry have you published?"

"Books of poetry? My poetry? I don't understand."

"Never mind. Where were you going when you were apprehended in Mirpur?"

"Jafarganj."

"Where is that?"

"About five miles west of Aricha."

"Is it a village?"

"A small one. It has a weekly market though. Saturdays and Tuesdays."

"What's your interest?"

"I don't know what you mean."

"What were you going there for? You are from India."

"No, I am not from India."

"But you told us that you were born in Burdwan, India."

"We used live there earlier. But we came to Dacca after the Partition in 1948."

"Oh yes. My mistake. Why Jafarganj?"

"My in-laws live there."

"You are married?"

"Yes."

"How long have you been married?"

"Eight years."

"Children?"

"Three."

"Why are they in Jafarganj while you are in Dacca?"

"I sent them there."

"When?"

"On the eighth of this month."

"On the eighth?"

"Yes, I sent them off by bus."

"Did you go to the meeting held on the seventh?"

"Which meeting?"

"The meeting at the Race Course Maidan?"

"Oh, yes, the meeting held by Sheikh Mujib."

"Did you attend it?"

"Yes."

"What is your profession? What work do you do?"

"I work for a firm."

"Government?"

"No, private."

"What else do you do?"

"Nothing."

"What about poetry?"

"Poetry? Whose poetry . . . "

"Don't you write poetry?"

At this point a soldier comes in through the door behind him, carrying a tray. As indicated by one of the officers, he places the tray in front of Nazrul. Nazrul extends his hand for the cup of tea on the tray, but stops when one of the officers raises his hand, as if to deny permission.

"D'you mean to say that you don't write poetry?"

"No, I don't."

"You've never written a poem?"

"Never."

"Never wanted to write one?"

"No, never."

Nazrul feels embarrassed, all of a sudden and hangs his head. "The truth is, I don't much understand poetry," he says.

"Ok, have your tea first."

Before raising the cup to his lips, Nazrul asks them, "will I be allowed to go home?"

"Of course you will."

Nazrul feels reassured and sips his tea. He even breaks off a piece of biscuit and puts it in his mouth. The piece breaks and crumbs roll down his lap. Nazrul sees the crumbs scattered on the floor and steals a guilty look around him. What will they think of him? But he finds all of them looking at him with gentle indulgence. He forgets about the biscuit and concentrates on the tea. Having emptied the cup he puts it gently back on the saucer, careful not to make a sound.

"What about the biscuit?"

Nazrul gives a guilty smile.

"Do you want another cup of tea?"

"No, no, this is enough."

"So you are Kazi Nazrul Islam."

"*Ji.*"

"And you have been in Dacca all this time, since 1948?"

"Yes."

"You sent your wife and children off to your in-laws' place?"

"Yes."

"On the eighth of March?"

"Yes."

"Who is cooking for you now?"

"Nobody. I am managing with food from a nearby restaurant. I can't cook and this is the arrangement when the family is away."

"So you've been spending your time mainly outside the house?"

"You can say that."

"Cigarette?"

"I beg your pardon?"

"Do you smoke?"

A packet of expensive, imported cigarettes is proffered, along with a matchbox.

"Have a cigarette."

As he opens the packet, Nazrul feels his hand trembling and thinks that the others in the room have noticed it too. Somehow he manages to light a cigarette, but is unable to draw properly on it. Something is choking his throat, something extending all the way to the pit of his stomach. The cigarette burns and begins to turn to ash between his fingers.

The flurry of questions resumes.

"So, you want to go to Jafarganj?"

"Yes. I would appreciate it if I can go today."

"Why?"

"They must be worrying about me."

What are they worrying about?

"Er, whether I am all right or not."

"You mean, whether you are alive or not."

"No, why should they think that I am dead?" Nazrul says quickly, afraid that any hint that he feared for his life would be taken amiss. He tries to draw himself up bravely and says, "I am not afraid of death."

"Why not?"

"Well, everybody has to die someday." The moment he says that, he has the horrible feeling that something has changed in the air. Something about what he just said has struck a discordant note, slamming an uncomfortable silence down into the center of the room. He steals a look at the file in front of the officers and lowers his eyes. Beads of sweat gather on his forehead but he cannot muster the courage to raise his hand to wipe them off.

One of his interrogators pushes his chair back with a screech and says, "we know that you do not fear death. But, just between friends, can I ask you something?"

Nazrul waits, the sweat now running down to his eyebrows.

"What did you do on the morning of the twenty-fifth of March?"

"The twenty-fifth of March?"

"Yes, try to remember. The morning of the twenty-fifth of March."

"Well, I woke up and made myself some tea."

"Then?"

"Then I went down to meet Bashir Sahib downstairs."

"Who is he?"

"The tenant who lives on the ground floor."

"What does he do?"

"Works somewhere, I think. I am not sure."

"You have stayed together for so long and yet you don't know where he works?"

"No. In any case he has been a tenant only for a couple of months.

His wife and mine have had differences from the outset about garbage being thrown from upstairs. Words were exchanged and we have never really been close."

"Yet you went to visit the same Bashir Sahib?"

"Yes, to read the newspaper. He gets the newspaper."

"And then?"

"I read the papers, chatted with Bashir Sahib briefly and came back upstairs."

"What did you chat about?"

"I don't remember very well now."

"Try to."

Suddenly, Nazrul is seized with fear and asks anxiously if Bashir Sahib had got into trouble.

"D'you think Bashir Sahib is the type of man who could get into trouble?"

"I don't know. Can't say." Nazrul is convinced that Bashir Sahib has been taken in by the authorities and this is the real reason behind his arrest at Mirpur Bridge. The man was obsessed with politics and missed no chance to discuss it with anybody he could catch hold of. No wonder he was in trouble.

"So?"

Suddenly Nazrul loses track of the conversation. "What did you discuss with Bashir Sahib?" The interlocutor repeats. Nazrul remembers shreds of the conversation he had with Bashir Sahib that day and is convinced that he will be released as soon as he provides an accurate report.

"Bashir Sahib was saying that Sheikh Mujib has taught Yahya such a lesson that the dictator was bound to relinquish power soon through a public proclamation and beat a cowardly retreat to Rawalpindi, never to return."

"What else did he talk about?"

"Oh yes, he also said that he didn't like the design of the liberation flag, especially the map of Bangladesh within the sun. He said that he has never seen a map inside the flag of any country."

"What else did the two of you talk about?"

"Well, he called out to his elder son, who was going out, to find out where he was going. The son said that he was going off to a demonstration near President's House. Bashir Sahib asked him to be careful but by then the son was out of earshot. Then he turned to me and said, 'it is this younger generation that is bringing freedom to the nation, while old folks like us have merely messed it up all these years with our policy of appeasement.'"

Nazrul lets the words tumble out without a pause and finally stops to take a deep breath. Then as further proof of what a dangerous character Bashir Sahib is, he adds, "He's asked me to go to demonstrations with him several times."

"Have you been with him? To demonstrations?"

"No."

It is a lie and Nazrul realizes that the tone of his voice has given him away. He has been to several such demonstrations and raised his voice in slogan with others, shouting, *Free us*! *Free Bangladesh*!

"You haven't been to any of them?"

Nazrul keeps quiet this time.

"Many poets have been to such demonstrations, haven't they?"

"Yes."

"Many writers too."

"Yes."

"What about you?"

"No, I've never been." This time the lie sounds a ring of truth in Nazrul's ears.

"I have never been to the processions. But Bashir Sahib has."

"What else?"

"I have no idea what else he might have done. I would have told you if I knew."

"I am not asking about Bashir Sahib. What did you do after you met him?"

"Oh. Well, I came back upstairs, maybe lay down for a bit and then got up to make the bed."

"Didn't you go to work?"

"Work? The office was shut."

"Why?"

"The owner closed the office down as soon as the decree for noncooperation was announced and he went off to Karachi on some business."

"And then?"

"As far as I know he is still in Karachi."

"Not him, what did you do then?"

"If I remember correctly, I went towards Sadarghat towards the afternoon. They were selling the '*Joy Bangla*' liberation flag there and I stopped to ask the price."

"Why?"

"Just on a whim. I wanted to find out at what price each size of flag was selling. I had no intention of buying one."

"Did you buy a flag finally?"

"No."

"Why not?"

"The landlord lives on the second floor of my house. He has put up a flag on the roof and that is good enough."

"And then?"

"I went looking for a cheap hotel at Sadarghat to eat lunch at. There are these cheap eating places on the boats at Sadarghat. Hindu eating places."

"Hindu eating places?"

"They serve rice and fish and people call them Hindu hotels."

"But you are Muslim, aren't you?"

"Yes, I am."

"And you still eat at eateries run by Hindus?"

"They are not really run by Hindus. It's just a name. They are run by Bengalis."

"So they are Bengali eateries?"

"Not even that. They just serve rice and fish."

"Just as Hindu ones do."

Nazrul feels like kicking himself. He had no business using the prefix 'Hindu.' And as if that was not bad enough, he has also let the word 'Bengali' slip out inadvertently. What if his interrogators find this reason enough to detain him further?

He's so scared now that the sweat drains from his face. He looks here and there furtively and notices that the fourth man in the room is waiting expectantly, his pencil poised over a notebook.

There is a long hiatus after which the questioning resumes.

"Fine, let's move on. What did you do next?"

A picture springs immediately to Nazrul's mind, a picture of two boys standing at the entrance to one of the eateries on the boats and shouting, "*Come, come, have a 'Joy Bangla' liberation lunch at half the price! Freedom is near and it's time to have rice and curry with big koi fish for a song. Come while stocks last!*" The two boys were taking turns to make their pitch in sing-song voices and Nazrul can still hear them. But he is not sure if he should mention this at all. In any case, since the questioning in the room is taking place in Urdu and Nazrul is replying in a strange hybrid version of the language, mixed with several English and Bengali words, it will be difficult for him to render an exact translation of their words.

"So which Hindu restaurant did you eat lunch at?"

"I didn't eat. I didn't have enough money. I just bought a packet of peanuts."

"So you didn't have lunch at all."

"No, later I did. At a friend's place."

"A friend from India?"

"Whom are you talking of?"

"The friend who gave you lunch."

"No, no why should he be from India? He too left Burdwan and came off to Dacca in '48 as I did. He's not been back since."

The fact is that Nazrul had lunched on the fish curry and rice being served at Sadarghat and can still remember how tasty the gravy had been. That was two days ago. The next day, the twenty-sixth, he could not leave his house because of the curfew and had to starve. The moment the curfew lifted on the morning of the twenty-seventh, he had set out for Jafarganj and had been arrested on the way. Since then, he has eaten nothing before drinking this cup of tea.

"What's the name of your friend who gave you lunch?"

Nazrul hesitates for a moment, not sure which name to give. Then he remembers Saleha and mentions her husband's name.

"Muhammmad Anisur Rahman."

"And what does he do?"

"He has a cycle-repair shop."

"Where?"

"At Banshal."

"Banshal is one of the strongholds of the liberationists, isn't it?"

Nazrul remains quiet. It is true that nearly every house in Banshal has a liberation flag fluttering from the roof. But the same is true of every locality in Dacca and he finds no reason for them to single out Banshal.

"Isn't it?"

"Maybe, I don't know. I really don't know." He pleads.

"So you went to Banshal and had lunch at your friend's. What time was that?"

"Around half past one or two."

"And after that?"

"Then I left Anisur Rahman Sahib's house."

Because all this is fiction, Nazrul tries hard to imagine himself leaving Anisur Rahman's house and going to Nawabpur—the place he had actually gone to from Sadarghat.

"And where did you go?"

"To Jinnah Avenue."

"What is the full name of Jinnah?"

"Nazrul is taken aback at this unexpected question."

"Say the full name."

"Muhammad Ali Jinnah."

"Doesn't he have the title Quaid-e-Azam before his name?"

"Yes, I forgot. Quaid-e-Azam Muhammad Ali Jinnah."

"Have you ever written a poem on the Quaid-e-Azam?"

"No."

"Any poem on Islamic ideals? On Pakistan?"

"No."

"Is it all right to write poems on Islamic ideals?"

"Of course."

"Then why have you never written one?"

"I never felt like writing a poem."

"On Islamic ideals?"

"No, generally. I have never felt like writing any poem."

"So, are we to take it that you, the poet Kazi Nazrul Islam, have been writing poems all this while against your wishes?"

"You are making a mistake. I have never written a single poem."

"Oh, so is it our mistake then?"

2

Nazrul realizes that no matter how he replies to that last question, he will be in trouble. He is still unable to understand why he is being subjected to such relentless yet pointless grilling.

"Anyway, if we are to believe you then you don't write poetry and have never written a single poem in your life. Now tell us what you did while you were at Jinnah Avenue."

Nazrul hesitates and replies, "I don't remember very well."

He really cannot remember because his mind has drifted and, in a sense, he is no longer present in the interrogation room. The only thing that troubles him is the question of why he is being subjected to this ordeal. How did he get here and what is the purpose behind his being here, when there is absolutely no reason for somebody like him to be in the same room with such men? He is not sure if it is not a strange dream after all.

"Well try to remember."

"I am trying."

"You were very cooperative until now. What happened all of a sudden? Do you want another cigarette?"

"A cigarette . . . yes."

Nazrul lights a fresh cigarette and his hand continues to tremble uncontrollably as before. The cigarette begins to burn between his fingers. He asks for a glass of water. When it comes he gulps down the water gratefully at one go.

"Kazi sahib, do you remember now?"

"Yes, I had been to Jinnah Avenue."

"You've told us that."

"Have I? Yes I have. I walked around there for a bit. I bumped into an old friend."

"Where?"

"Near the stadium."

"Who is this friend?"

"He works in a bookshop."

"A bookshop, did you say?"

"Yes a bookshop selling school textbooks. I go there sometimes to look him up."

"Does the shop sell poetry books?"

"Maybe. It also sells imported books."

"Do your books of poetry sell there too?"

"My poetry? How can they? I haven't published a single book of poetry."

"Answer the question you are asked and don't question us."

Nazrul is taken aback at the curtness of the reply and a chill descends upon him, as if the chair he is sitting on has been taken away and he is sitting merely on a chair-shaped void.

"What's the name of the friend?"

"Osman."

"And what did Osman tell you?"

"He told me that the Bengalis are making a grave mistake. Sheikh Mujib has betrayed them and is leading them astray. He said a few other things in the same vein."

"As you stood on the road?"

"Yes."

"Were you annoyed with him?"

"Me?"

"Weren't you annoyed with him when he said that?"

Nazrul isn't sure which way the conversation is going and replies guardedly, "no."

"Then how did you feel?"

"Well, I weighed his words and deliberated on them to see if Osman was correct or not."

"And what conclusion did you come to?"

"He could be right. Osman keeps track of what's going on around him. You see, many different people come to the bookstore and talk with him."

Nazrul is now keen to blame the treason on anyone he happens to speak of, so that he can secure his own release and be on the way to Jafarganj.

"Anyway, I said goodbye to Osman soon and walked off."

"In which direction?"

"Towards Ramna Park. It was a hot day and I felt like going to the park to sit in the open."

"Then?"

"I sat in the park till it grew dark. It crossed my mind that I should return home and so I did."

"Then?"

"There was some *chira* in the house and I polished it off with some sugar. Then I went to bed."

"What time was that?"

"I don't know. My wristwatch had stopped working, I think. But it couldn't have been later than nine or nine-thirty."

"How come you went off to sleep without waiting for the proclamation?"

"What proclamation?"

"Didn't Bashir Sahib tell you that the President was ready to relinquish power that very day and leave? Weren't you curious about that? Didn't you switch on the radio even once to listen to the bulletin?"

"I don't have a radio."

"Well, nothing stopped you from going to Bashir Sahib's place."

"He wasn't home."

"So you did go to him?"

"No, I saw him leaving when I was returning home."

"Then?"

"I must have gone off to sleep."

"Do you sleep early?"

"Quite early. I wake up early too. I have to go to market in the morning and then to the office."

"What happened then?"

"What do you suppose? I set off towards Mirpur bridge once the curfew lifted . . . "

"We'll come to that later. What did you do when you woke up the next morning?"

"It was still dark when I woke up."

"Why? What woke you up?"

Nazrul's voice drops to a whisper as he replies, "the sound of firing."

"Have you heard the sound before?"

"Yes, I have."

"Where?"

"In films."

"So you could make out the sound of firing even in your sleep?"

"Not at first, no."

"When did you make out?"

"Soon."

"What time was it?"

"It was still dark. Maybe ten past eleven."

"How did you know that was the exact time? You said your wristwatch wasn't working."

"I have an alarm clock which showed the time."

"But you didn't feel like checking the time when you went to sleep?"

"The clock is actually in the next room."

"So once you heard the sound of firing, you went to the next room?"

"Yes."

"Why? There was no one in the house, was there?"

"Actually, one can see the main road from the next room. I wanted to see where the sound of gunfire was coming from."

"And could you see?"

"No."

"What did you do next?"

"I switched off all the lights and sat on my bed quietly."

"Immediately?"

"Yes, immediately."

"Have a cigarette."

"But before Nazrul can light another cigarette he is interrupted by another question."

"Tell me, what thoughts crossed your mind when you heard the sound of gunfire?"

"I could make out the firing was heavy."

"No. Please listen to the question carefully and answer. Who did you think were firing?"

Nazrul is unsure of what answer to give. The moment he had heard the shots, the thought had crossed his mind that the military could be firing on marching students. Nazrul never believed those who used to say that the army was cowering in fear inside the cantonment, because he himself was a timid man by nature. Fear was a natural instinct with him and what scared him most were weapons and those who had the power to wield them.

He debates over whether to suggest that the Bengalis were firing guns, because that could make things even more awkward for him. For one, he may be asked how he could be sure that the Bengalis were armed. For another, they might believe that he was privy to the activities of the liberationists and pester him to confess what he knew about their armaments and hideouts.

"What did you think?"

Nazrul hesitates as before and then decides it would be best to speak the truth.

"I imagined that the students must have crossed a line and your troops had therefore been forced to open fire."

"What else did you think?"

"I was afraid, very afraid."

"Why? Nobody was firing on you or your locality."

"I was worried for my family."

"But your family is out of Dacca."

"Still, I worried for them."

"Were you worried that the Bengalis might lose this battle?"

"No."

"Were you worried that *we* might have to beat a retreat?"

"That thought didn't cross my mind."

"So you were worried about your family, that's all."

"Yes, I told you so."

"Did the fear persist the next day?"

"Yes."

"Did you listen to the President's speech on the radio the next day?"

"I did."

"But you don't have a radio."

"Bashir Sahib has one."

"So you went to his place and listened to the speech on his radio?"

"Yes, I did."

"Did you hear of Mujib's arrest?"

"Yes."

"Did that news make you more afraid or less? Please answer. What was your reaction?"

"I was afraid."

"Why?"

"For my wife. For my children. I would have been fine had they been with me. Please believe me, I am worried only for them. I neither understand nor enjoy politics. I didn't even vote during the elections, because I was down with fever. I try to steer clear of marches or strikes because I don't want to get shot. I can't stand the sight of blood, which is why I did not opt for the medical profession after passing the ISC. I can't think beyond my family and that's why I was afraid."

Nazrul feels tears rolling down his cheeks and is stung by embarrassment. He could never have imagined that he would weep before a roomful of strangers. But he also finds relief in his tears, in the thought that they might take pity on him and release him after all.

"Yet you, the same you, are so fearless in your poems!"

The three officers stare at Nazrul, their eyes blazing with scorn.

3

Nazrul stares at them uncomprehendingly, his eyes dimmed by tears. Soon one of the officers thrusts a printed piece of paper at him. Nazrul blinks once or twice to clear his eyes. He recognizes that the paper he is holding in his hand is a snippet he himself had cut out of a newspaper a few days back.

The top half of the paper carries a picture of the liberation flag with '*Joy Bangla*' written above it. Below it are two lines of poetry, translated into English:

Raise your voices as one, and sing!
The flag of tomorrow flies high
'Pon the nor'wester's wing.

A few more lines are followed by the name 'Kazi Nazrul Islam,' written in large letters.

In a flash everything becomes clear to Nazrul. His jailers have mistaken him for the famous scion of Burdwan, the renowned poet Kazi Nazrul Islam, after whom he has been named. A ludicrous case of mistaken identity is behind his captivity, though he could never have imagined that anyone would ever take him for the famous poet. Nazrul feels relieved as soon as he has worked this out. He will now quickly set their confusion to rest and secure his own release.

Nazrul begins to laugh, loudly, audibly. "You have made a big mistake," he tells them as he laughs, "Nazrul the poet of revolt, is older, much older than me. He is also not quite right in the head and lives in Calcutta. I am not the same man. Your soldiers made a mistake, do you get me?"

A resounding slap lands on his cheek, which begins to burn as though a burning torch has been pressed against it. Hot tears of pain brim in his eyes once again.

The slaps do not cease and his face is struck repeatedly, alternately on the left and the right, till it feels numb all over.

Between each slap, the officer on the left who has come up to him, says, "We haven't made a mistake. We don't make mistakes, do you hear me, Mr Poet? We were treating you with respect all this time because you are a poet. But now we see that you are not only a traitor to the state, but a liar too. You thought you were too smart for us, didn't you? Did you think you could fool us and give us the slip?"

Nazrul blacks out and falls off the chair to the floor. When the officer lands a sharp kick on his stomach, his body arches once like a bow and then grows still. The officer issues a sharp command for him to be taken away.

4

Nazrul opens his eyes and finds himself back in his cell. The light is so bright that he is forced to shut his eyes immediately. The room, large and threatening one moment, reduces to a small pin-prick of light the next.

After a long time he opens his eyes slowly once again. This time he notices a bright light, powerful like the sun, placed on a three-legged stool at the same level as his eyes. He does not remember seeing this light before.

He tries to get up but finds that he cannot move. His legs are tied to the bed and he is handcuffed. His body is drenched in sweat and there is a bitter taste in his mouth. When he tries to spit, stale blood comes out.

He collapses back upon the bed, the world around him rent by the macabre laughter of the insanity that reigns over it.

What else can explain the events that have taken place since the night of the twenty-fifth? What else, but insanity can explain a modern, well-trained army swooping down upon sleeping citizens in the dead of the night, setting fire to marketplaces and reducing entire colonies to rubble with shelling? He can no longer think coherently. He can feel his lips and ears swollen from blows and his chin wet with the blood that has trickled down to it from one ear. He can still smell the pungent odor of gunpowder floating in the air of his city.

He remembers the large crowds running helter-skelter, silently, like insects whose dens have been destroyed. Not a sound could be heard anywhere, yet a heart-rending cry appeared to course from one end of the city to the other. He remembers someone telling him that the only bus leaving for Aricha could be found near Mirpur Bridge. All roads on this side were closed. That was when he had started off towards Mirpur Bridge.

As he neared Mirpur Bridge he had seen a row of soldiers blocking the approach, telling citizens to go back to the city since there was nothing to fear. Those who still wanted to venture forward were being stopped for questioning. He remembers carrying a small suitcase which is missing now and which they had ordered him to open. Then they had searched his pockets and found the piece of paper with the poem. A soldier had inspected it and asked him for his name. As he was giving them his name he had noticed the name Kazi Nazrul Islam written below the poem. When they arrested him he had not been able to understand why he was being taken into custody, though now he knows why. But he can still not understand how such a mistake can be made. The probable has moved into the realm of the possible and the city he has known so well has turned overnight into a place where anything, no matter how unlikely, can come true.

The door opens to bring in a new officer whom he has not seen before. When Nazrul tries to get up the officer silently indicates with a gesture that he should remain lying on the bed. A soldier brings a chair into the room. The officer pulls the chair up next to Nazrul's bed with a quiet smile on his face, as if he is an old friend come for a chat.

Nazrul gives him a terror-stricken look and says, "please believe me, I am not the poet Kazi Nazrul Islam. It will be obvious if you make inquiries. There has been a big mistake. The real Nazrul is much older than me and lives in Calcutta. He also suffers from mental illness. I am not the man you are looking for."

The officer ignores the issue and simply observes, "why, they seem to have beaten you up!"

Nazrul chooses to stay quiet about the beating because he does not wish to invite fresh trouble.

"They seem to have beaten you up badly. You are bleeding from your ear. This is unfair, very unfair. How could they do this to someone like you? Shame!"

He calls a soldier and orders Nazrul's handcuffs to be removed. The soldier obeys immediately.

"Now get a bucket of water. Quick."

A bucket of water appears and the officer tells Nazrul to wash his face. Although he has no desire to do so, the pleasing behavior of the officer reassures him that they have discovered their mistake and his incarceration will now end.

"Will I be able to see my children? He asks the officer."

"Surely."

"I wish to go to Jafarganj."

"You will be taken there."

"When?"

"Whenever you want to go."

Nazrul cannot believe that they will let him go so easily.

"Can I . . . can I go now?"

"Yes you can."

"Then . . . then . . . "

Nazrul cannot decide whether he should get up and walk to freedom through the door or not. The officer makes no move either to encourage or dissuade him. He simply inquires if Nazrul is feeling any pain.

Nazrul lies that although he had been in pain earlier, now he is fine.

"Did they put some medicine on your wounds?"

"No."

The officer shakes his head and says, "they should have." Nazrul looks at him eagerly, waiting for him to say that he can now go. But the officer remains silent. Suddenly there is a scream outside, as if a skewer has been run through someone's throat. But the scream stops the next moment. Nazrul looks worriedly at the door and licks his cracked lips nervously.

"It's nothing. They've caught someone red-handed." The officer explains gently.

"What was he doing?"

"Sending messages by wireless across the border. These are the real enemies of the state and they have to be punished. What do you say?"

Nazrul feels uncomfortable but hopes that he, at least, is no longer being considered an enemy of the state. "May I go?" He asks, unsurely.

"Of course, you may. There is just a small formality to be taken care of."

"What's that?"

"You have to sign a document and then your ordeal will be over. If you want, we can take you wherever you want to go. Or, we can bring your family back to Dacca. Your choice."

"I wish to go."

"Where?"

"To Jafarganj."

"Where's Jafarganj?"

"A few miles west of Aricha."

"But we can bring them back to Dacca."

"I haven't been to Jafarganj in a while. So I'd rather go."

The officer continues to look at him benignly and says in a gentle voice, "you don't want to stay in Dacca any longer, do you?"

"It's not that. Please understand that Dacca has been my home since 1948 and I really like living here. I can't bear the thought of living anywhere else."

"Then why do you want to go?"

"I want to see my wife and children."

"But it's not even been a month since they've been gone."

"That's right."

"And we can bring them back here. In which case, you needn't leave town at all."

"No, I needn't."

"Or are you afraid that the military is going to massacre the citizenry?"

"No. No, I don't apprehend anything like that."

"Then what are you thinking?"

Nazrul is unable to furnish a reply and gives a vacant stare. He gives a start when he notices the officer looking at him with a steady, inquisitive gaze.

"You don't want to tell me?"

"It's not that."

"Can't you tell me? I think the fact is that you can't trust me, though I am merely trying to get you free. Why am I doing that? Because I hold poets in high esteem."

"But I am not the poet you think I am."

"We know you are. Is it right that you should deny it? Aren't you well known? Don't the papers print your poems on the front page?"

"I am not the same man."

"You are and it behooves a poet like you to speak out the truth."

"I am not hiding anything."

"No?"

"No."

"Hmm . . . and I had thought you would be at least as fearless as the poems you write."

"I didn't write those poems."

"I would have thought that you would be the one Bengali who is not afraid to speak truthfully."

"But I am telling you the truth."

At this point, a soldier enters to hand the officer a heavy, official-looking folder. The officer takes out a sheet of paper from the folder and hands Nazrul a pen.

"Please sign this statement."

5

He has no idea of how much time passes, because he loses track of all time. An hour or two? A day and a night? Or is it a week that has gone by? All he knows is that he has been lying on the bed for a long time, his body limp with hunger and pain, till magically his head clears and he feels normal once again. He can no longer feel any pain or pangs of hunger.

Opening his eyes he can see a narrow crack running across the ceiling from which the bright light is suspended. He finds that the cuffs have been taken off and he can sit up on the bed easily enough, though he continues to lie upon it.

A sudden question pops up in his head like a bird leaving its nest to take flight. Could he have actually put his signature to that statement if he had indeed been the poet Kazi Nazrul Islam?

The familiar, stylized signature of the poet, which he has seen many times in books, emerges before his eyes and he cannot imagine it being affixed beneath that statement full of lies.

Nazrul tries to get up but his head begins to swim and his back aches from an old pain. He utters a muffled cry and crashes back upon the bed. One by one the words float before his eyes—Nazrul, Nazrul Islam, Kazi Nazrul Islam, Kazi Nazrul Islam the poet of rebellion, Nazrul the Rebellious, Nazrul. It is this last word which gains in size till it appears to cover his vision completely.

A new question enters his mind gradually, as daylight enters a darkened room. *How does one write a poem*? *A P-O-E-M*? When he named his son Nazrul, had his father hoped that the son would grow up to be a poet some day? But how did one write a poem, letter by letter, word by word, each line strung out in a meter and rhyming with the next?

The words written on the newspaper cutting he had put in his pocket explode inside his brain.

Raise your voices as one, and sing!
Raise your voices as one, and sing!
Raise your voices as one, and sing!

Nazrul sits up straight on the bed.

The flag of tomorrow flies high
'Pon the nor'wester's wing

The poem arranges itself before his eyes, line by line, stanza by stanza.

With a loud crash the door opens and before he knows it, two khaki-clad figures pounce on him. A hailstorm of kicks and blows begins to rain upon him till he loses count of time. But like every other torture, this too comes to an end and he is cast upon the floor and left to bleed, alive and conscious.

As he lies there, without attempting to get up, Nazrul finds that he has become a stranger unto himself and is beginning to find the entire situation amusing. Dwelling on the comedy of errors that has led to his being mistaken for another man, he feels laughter erupting in every part of his brain—loud, uncontrollable guffaws that slowly take his consciousness away from him.

When he wakes up he is reminded again of Saleha.

6

He can see her clearly, Saleha with her dark eyes and dimpled chin, as clearly as in a photograph stuck to the wall of his cell. Saleha's father had been a music tutor who used to coach students at their homes after he shifted to Dacca from Burdwan. A fellow-student of Nazrul used to take lessons from him and Saleha's father would come to their house every afternoon, taking care to first fold the umbrella he would carry and keep it gently in a corner. Then, with an almost comical leap, he would climb on to the bed and begin to play the harmonium. His name was Alauddin and by nature he was cautious and circumspect in his movements as if he did not wish to disturb the order of the universe unduly. But the same man would be transformed whenever he sat next to the harmonium to make music and all his patience would seem to desert him immediately.

"What happened now, Samad Miyan?" He would demand, "Come quickly and catch this tune, will you?" With his neck bent to one side and his eyes closed, he would gently guide his student into the notes of the *saregama*. He was intolerant of any mistakes made during practice and his fury at such moments belied the otherwise peaceable nature he exhibited.

Before he left each day, he would sing a couple of songs by himself, one of which Nazrul remembered for a long time afterwards:

Wherefore do you brood alone in the wild?
Come with us to fetch water, O fair child.

As he sang, his voice would ring with a sad pleading note which would resonate with his listeners in the deepest corner of the spirit.

The first time Nazrul saw the teenaged Saleha was when he accompanied Samad to visit the tutor when the latter fell ill. As soon as he saw her it struck him that Saleha surely was made in the image of the 'fair child' whose friends importuned her not to brood alone but go fetch water with them.

He began to visit the tutor in his house, without Samad, on the pretext of taking music lessons, though the real attraction was Saleha. He took lessons for a few years till one day, when he was sitting with Saleha, waiting for the tutor who was away, she asked him, "Why do you make such an effort to sing, when you know very well that you don't have a talent for music? My father doesn't say anything because he needs the money, but surely Allah has given you ears sharp enough to know that you can't sing."

Nazrul had reddened and stopped taking tuition. When Saleha was getting married Alauddin Sahib had paid him a visit to invite him to the ceremony. Nazrul felt a stab of pain in his breast when he took the card. At that moment he realized that he had been besotted with Saleha. Saleha was the first and practically the only love of his life.

Nazrul sits up, the putrid smell of urine all around and a bucket filled with his own vomit placed next to him. His body heaves with a spasm of nausea and though his intestines begin to churn, he cannot throw up any more. Beads of sweat appear in his forehead and he feels so thirsty that he begins to suck on his forefinger. But he can barely quench his thirst that way. He gets to his feet and totters like a drunken man to the door. He begins to hammer on the door and scream. He is surprised and repelled by the weak, cracked voice that emerges from his throat, as if his vocal cords have been stretched and ripped like a rag.

Nobody comes to open the door and soon he slumps next to it, unable to hammer any more. He tries to estimate how long he has lain imprisoned in his cell but the moment he tries to think his head is racked with pain. How does one write a poem? Could he have written a poem for Saleha and expressed his love for her, instead of letting her go to another man? Did a humble clerk like Kazi Nazrul Islam, the refugee from Burdwan, have it in him to express his anguish and love in poetic terms?

He feels like relieving himself but even after he tries for a long time not a single drop of urine emerges.

The door opens and a couple of khakis come in. Grasping him firmly, they haul him to his feet and drag him out of the cell to a new interrogation room. He is made to sit on a new chair and soon a third khaki comes to sit opposite him and asks him solicitously if he is all right.

"*Paani . . . paani . . .* " Nazrul can only mumble for water.

A polished metal glass full of clear water is brought before him, cold droplets sticking to the metallic surface. Nazrul tries to grab it, but someone holds him firmly from the back and he barely manages to steal a sip before the glass is whisked away from his lips.

"Have you changed your mind?" The new khaki asks Nazrul. "Are you willing to sign the statement now?"

"Sign? Statement?"

The statement is thrust before him and Nazrul remembers everything that has gone on before.

"I am not Nazrul Islam."

"You are a liar."

"No, you are making a mistake. I am not the same man."

"Don't lie to us."

"I am telling you the truth. A clenched fist crashes into his chest."

"Do you still mean to say that you are not Nazrul Islam?"

"I am not." Nazrul has no idea just how he can make them understand. It would be easy enough to cave in to their demands and put his signature to the statement. The torture would stop and he would be released. He cannot fathom who or what is stopping him from signing the document, providing him with immense strength to put up with the brutal torture.

All of a sudden he feels at ease. He forgets that he is starving and his body appears to recover completely from the beating. When his interrogator lights a cigarette and stares at him, exhaling a stream of smoke in his face, Nazrul too, stares back, his eyes locked with those of the man before him in a silent act of defiance.

Something rumbles across the road outside like a roll of thunder, making the window panes shiver as it passes by. All of a sudden the questioning resumes.

"Haven't you incited the Bengalis to rebellion?"

Nazrul is silent.

"Didn't you urge them to take up arms for the cause of liberation?"

Nazrul stares back placidly, surprised at his own nonchalance. A second self within him seems to be controlling his actions and he feels only the urge to obey the commands of that unseen self.

"Haven't you written songs fomenting unrest?"

Nazrul stares back steadily, like a hypnotized man.

"Aren't you Nazrul Islam?"

"No."

"No?"

The interrogator grabs Nazrul's hand and presses the burning cigarette against the flesh. A smell of burning skin fills the room. The khaki stubs the cigarette out against Nazrul's arm and then gives a silent command to the two sentries, who grab his hair and pull him up to his feet. Then they push him back to the chair and repeat the action. Again and again.

For a moment, everything grows dark before Nazrul's eyes. When he comes back to his senses the face of the interrogator, thrust close to his, appears to be large and leering, an amused look flitting across it from time to time.

"Do you think your wife will recognize you when you go back to her? Maybe it's better not to see her again. What do you say?"

Nazrul starts because he has forgotten about his wife. His reaction does not escape the interrogator who continues, "and your children? Do you really want to scar their impressionable minds forever by showing them this battered face of yours? Better to die, don't you think?"

The arm on which the cigarette had been stubbed smarts with pain.

"Fine, you will be allowed to die if you so wish. But it won't be the death of a patriot. The Bengalis won't hail you as a martyr; in fact they will simply say that the poet Kazi Nazrul Islam was a dangerous reactionary who was trying to delude them with false promises before betraying them. They will spit on your memory, calling you a despicable enemy of the people."

"No. They will say he was a rebel."

The interrogator looks visibly taken aback.

"So you admit that you are a rebel?"

"Not me. Nazrul."

"Aren't you the same man?"

"No! No! How many times do I have to tell you that?" Nazrul manages to shout before hands are clapped upon his mouth. The hailstorm of kicks and blows resumes upon his battered and bruised body.

When he regains consciousness, he is asked the same question. "Aren't you the poet Nazrul?"

"No."

They pounce upon him again till he is knocked out cold. Every time he comes round, he is asked the same question. His answer remains the same as before and the beating renews with fresh ferocity.

7

Is it day or night outside? The innocuous question pops up in his mind as Nazrul loses consciousness once again. This is because a great gulf now separates his body and his soul, as if, completely dissociated from the other, each is possessed of an identity of its own.

When he wakes up he finds himself seated on a chair. For a moment he wonders if he is at a hairdresser's saloon for a shave and has merely nodded off.

"Are you claiming to speak the truth?"

"Yes" I am telling you the truth." His own voice seems muffled and strange as if he is speaking with his head shoved inside a bucket.

"Don't you ever lie?"

"I am not lying to you." Nazrul replies mechanically, without even trying to open his eyes and see what his present interlocutor (and tormentor) looks like. He does not feel the need to do so.

"Who is Nazrul Islam?"

"I am."

"But you don't write poetry."

"No."

"Then whose poem got published in the newspaper on the twenty-fifth of March?"

"Nazrul Islam's."

"Not yours?"

"No."

"Did you read the newspaper on the twenty-fifth?"

"Yes."

"And you cut out the portion of the paper with the poem on it. Why?"

"I don't know. I can't remember."

"Wasn't it because the poem had been written by you?"

"No."

"Do you remember the poem?"

"Not very well. A few lines maybe."

"Try to recite it."

"*Raise your voices as one and sing . . . the flag of tomorrow flies high 'pon the nor'wester's wing* . . . and then . . . *come with us to fetch water, o fair child* . . . no, this line is from a song. I don't remember any more of the poem."

"Do you remember the day of the twenty-fifth of March?"

Nazrul is quiet.

"Do you remember what you did the whole day?"

Nazrul has a feeling that he was asked the same question before. That time too, he had replied in the hope that they would let him go.

"What did you do when you woke up in the morning?"

"Is it morning now?"

"The morning of the twenty-fifth. What did you do when you got up?"

"Read the newspaper."

"Then?"

"Read that poem. Then I went out to do some shopping. No, not that day, that was some other day."

"Then?"

"I cut the poem out and put it in my pocket."

"Then?"

"I had tea with Bashir Sahib."

"Who lives downstairs? You didn't make tea for yourself?"

"I can't remember."

"You seem to be pretty quick with your answers."

"Will you release me if I answer all your questions?"

"Do you wish to be released?"

"Yes, but don't ask me to sign a statement."

"Why not?"

"Because I am not Nazrul Islam."

"What did Bashir Sahib tell you when you were having tea?"

"Nothing."

"Nothing?"

"I can't remember whether he said anything or not."

"Try to remember."

"I am very hungry."

"What did Bashir Sahib say?"

"I am in terrible pain."

"What conversation did you have with Bashir Sahib?"

"He told me that we are soon going to be free. Yahya is going to give up power and leave."

He is slapped on the face. He opens his eyes, surprised that he has been hit even though he is answering them obediently.

"Yahya is not some pal of yours. He is the president of this country."

Nazrul understands why he has been slapped and closes his eyes again.

"Did Bashir Sahib say anything about the '*Joy Bangla*' flag of liberation?"

"The flag of liberation?"

"Yes, the flag about which you wrote that poem."

"I wrote a poem? About the flag?"

"Try to remember what Bashir Sahib said."

"I think he had a flag stitched at home. He didn't buy one."

"Answer the question."

"I am trying."

"When did you leave the house?"

"In the morning."

"Where did you go?"

"To Sadarghat."

"Why?"

"To eat rice and fish."

"Where?"

"At an eatery. An eatery on a boat."

"A Hindu eatery?"

"I am very hungry. Famished."

"You ate rice and fish there?"

"Please give me something to eat."

"Answer us and you will be given food."

"Please, let me have something to eat at least. Anything."

"Tell us the truth first."

"I am speaking the truth."

"No they are all lies."

"Believe me, I am very hungry."

"Speak the truth and don't try to be smart."

"I am not trying to be smart."

"Then why have you been telling us lies all this while? Why are your answers conflicting with your previous versions?"

Nazrul screams, leaps to his feet though he barely has any strength left to stand straight and topples to the floor. As he tries to scramble up on all fours like a beaten animal, he yells, "Kill me! Finish me off!"

8

But this time he does not lose consciousness. He feels a couple of drops of urine drip unbidden down his thigh. He can clearly see three pairs of eyes fixing him with a steady gaze.

"Didn't you visit the liberationists in their stronghold on the twenty-fifth?"

"I have no idea where their stronghold is."

"Didn't you urge them to launch their attack the same night?"

"No."

"Did none of the rebels alert you that an attack on the armed forces was being planned for the same night?"

"I don't know any rebels."

"Who are their ringleaders?"

"I don't know."

"Do you know of their whereabouts?"

"No."

"But we are sure that you are well acquainted with them."

"You are making a mistake."

"You are the one who is making a mistake and inviting his own death upon himself. We are being patient and sensitive with you because you are a poet. I repeat, do you know the ringleaders?"

"I have told you, I don't."

"Very well, even if you don't tell us, we know who they are. Now we want you to tell them to surrender. We also want you to sign this statement and let the common people know how these dangerous liberationists are gambling their future away. That's all you have to do."

Nazrul remains silent.

"Sign here."

"I am not the poet Nazrul Islam."

"Then simply sign as Nazrul Islam. That'll do."

Nazrul extends his hand and a pen is placed into it. Somebody spreads the document out before his eyes.

"If I sign will you let me go?"

"Certainly."

"Will I be allowed to go to Jafarganj?"

"We'll escort you there."

"Will I be able to see my family again?"

"Yes, you will."

Nazrul puts pen to paper and is about to sign when his hand begins to tremble violently, as if shaken by someone else inside him. He finds it difficult to hold the pen steady and hears a voice whisper in his ears, the moment you put your signature on that paper, it will become the poet's signature. Unable to ignore the persistent whisper he looks in bewilderment at the faces around him. The pen drops from his hand. Nazrul emits a garbled cry and faints.

He is woken up by water being splashed on his face. His parched tongue slips out of his mouth like a snake in search of the cold touch of water. But the moment it feels the touch, the deep thirst within him seems to emerge from his breast like a big bird with fluttering wings.

"Will you sign?"

At first he cannot make out the words.

"Will you sign here?"

He shakes his head silently.

"Do you want to drink some *paani*?"

He nods.

A long pipe is dragged into the room. A couple of men grab him and press him to the floor before the pipe is pushed into his mouth. Nazrul lies quietly with the pipe in his mouth, almost as if he is rehearsing for a play.

All of a sudden water begins to gush out of the pipe and enter his mouth and throat with great force. Nazrul gives a gut-wrenching hiccup and tries to spit the pipe out of his mouth, but in vain. The gurgling water pours into his stomach and swells it up. When his first child was being born, Nazrul had pressed his ear against the similarly distended tummy of his pregnant wife to listen to the heartbeat of the unborn infant.

When they finally remove the pipe he is gasping for breath. With so much water inside him he feels like vomiting. He tries to get up but they force him down to the floor and a few of them press on his stomach with their feet till all the water begins to come out again through his mouth, nose and even his ears.

For a minute he loses his senses.

When he recovers, he finds himself drenched and lying in a pool of water on the floor. He is panting so hard that he is unable to think cogently.

The image of his wife flashes before his eyes and he is glad that he had the sense not to marry another friendless, kinless refugee like himself. His wife would at least be safe with her brothers at Jafarganj. He himself is now certain of his own death and no longer afraid of it.

The paper containing the written statement is waved once more before his eyes and he is asked if he will sign.

He shakes his head vigorously.

"Think again."

"No. No."

"They are going to pour water into your mouth again, mind you."

"Let them."

Once again he is subjected to the same torture. A jet of water pours out of the pipe to flood his stomach, after which unknown men stand on it to make him regurgitate all the water out. This time he remains unconscious for a long time.

The paper with the statement is idly folded into the shape of a bird or an airplane and launched through the window, never to return.

Nazrul thinks his wife is standing near him. He tries to tell her at the top of his voice, "*Get out of here. Don't come near this putrid hell, filled with water.*" But she refuses and remains standing by his side. "*Do you remember,*" she asks him.

"*What?*"

"*The first day?*"

"*What first day?*"

"*The day we got married? Do you remember that day?*"

"*Yes, I do.*"

"*What date was it?*"

"*The twenty-fifth of March.*"

"*No, you are wrong. Try to remember again.*"

"*I am trying . . . trying.*"

"*What was the date of our marriage?*"

"*I remember now. The first of June.*"

"*What was I wearing?*"

"*I can't remember.*"

"*Try.*"

"*You wore a red sari.*"

"*Every bride wears a red sari on the day of her marriage. The truth is that you have forgotten everything and are making things up.*"

"*Why are you grilling me like them?*" Nazrul asks piteously.

"*Because you've forgotten everything, that's why.*"

"*What have I forgotten?*"

"*You've forgotten me.*"

Nazrul stares at her face silently. Her face is so close to his that he can almost touch it with his hand.

"*Why did you come here, Kumkum?*"

"*I had to come because you seem to have forgotten everything.*"

"*What?*"

"*Don't you remember what you said on our wedding night when you drew me close and whispered in my ear?*"

"*I remember, Kumkum.*"

"*Then say it.*"

"*I had said that I would never leave you or cause you any grief. We would take the rough with the smooth together and share our pain.*"

"*Now you remember.*"

"*Why did you come here?*"

"*Because you are forgetting your promise. You are going away and leaving me in grief. You are no longer ready to share my pain.*"

"*Kumkum, go away, please.*"

"*Look at me, Nazrul.*"

"*No.*"

"*Tell me why you are deserting me this way.*"

"*Don't stay here Kumkum. This is hell. Can't you smell the stench of the water? Go away.*" Nazrul shouts and opens his eyes. He is alone in the room. He shuts his eyes again. When he opens them next he can see Kumkum, weeping inconsolably with her head resting on the door-frame.

"*Are you crying, Kumkum?*"

Kumkum gives no reply.

"*Are you crying?*"

Nazrul turns his face to the window and finds Kumkum there, her body quivering with silent sobs as she presses her face to the window.

"*Are you crying?*"

Kumkum vanishes only to reappear standing against a vast, barren wall and crying.

Nazrul closes his eyes. The vision of Kumkum goes away.

He can hear his children calling him from far away, "*A-b-b-o-o!*"

"*Go away. Don't come near me.*"

"*Abbu!*"

"*Listen to me. Go.*"

The children's voices cease. Nazrul sits up, resting his weight on his elbow and begins to pant. The door opens.

"I am a doctor."

Nazrul narrows his eyes to see the man clearly. He can only make out a figure filling a syringe with deep concentration.

"Give me your hand."

"You are a doctor?"

"Yes."

"Am I still alive, then?"

9

"Am I still alive, doctor?"

"Of course you are."

"Is this an injection you are giving me?"

"Yes, it is. You'll be fine afterwards."

"Wait!"

A grim command is issued near the door. The doctor turns to the speaker who comes forward with slow, measured steps.

"Move away, doctor." The speaker stares straight at Nazrul and says, in a terrifying voice, "listen carefully."

Nazrul tries but can only hear the sound of a shrill whistle in his ears. After a long time the whistle stops.

The newcomer brings his mouth close to Nazrul's ear and whispers, "do you know what's in that syringe?"

"No."

"Do you want to know? That syringe contains germs, germs that spread cancer."

"Ca-cancer?"

"Yes. Once it enters your body you'll never be cured."

"No?"

"No. There's no cure for cancer."

"No?"

"No. The blood will drain from your body and you will perish bit by bit, experiencing excruciating agony."

"I don't want to die."

"I know that."

"I want to live."

"I know that you want to live."

"Please, please save me."

The man gives a faint smile and replies, "I am glad that I came just in time. I am not going to let a poet like you die a dog's death. Never. You'll be fine and write many more poems."

"I am not Nazrul Islam."

"You will be the new Nazrul Islam. We want a new poet by that name. Not the old one."

The doctor makes a silent exit. The newcomer switches off the bright light and turns on a dimmer lamp. The room fills with a mellow glow.

"You won't have to suffer any more. No more suffering for you. I am making the necessary arrangements," he says.

Nazrul is taken to another room where his body is wiped clean with a warm towel. He is dressed in fresh clothes and given a cup of hot milk to drink. Nazrul holds the cup with both hands and drinks the milk in one gulp silently. The next moment he brings it all up.

The mess is cleared by a silent attendant and he is helped back to the bed. Everyone leaves the room except the concerned newcomer who pulls up a chair next to him.

"Where is Kumkum?" Nazrul asks in a faint voice.

"Who is Kumkum?"

"My wife. I thought I heard Khokon, my son and Mamata, my daughter. I saw Kumkum too. Where are they?"

"Where did you see them?"

"Inside the room."

"They are not here. You are imagining things. But we have found out that they are fine."

"Are they all right? Did you check?"

"Of course we checked. You will see for yourself when you meet them."

"Will I be allowed to go?"

"Yes of course."

"I won't be able to sign any documents, though."

"You won't have to."

"No?" Nazrul is surprised.

"You don't have to put your signature to any statement. That was torn up long ago. This is the problem with the younger officers. They don't know how to behave with people."

"I don't have to sign any statement?"

"I told you so. But . . . you'll just have to write a poem."

"A poem?"

"Yes. Just one."

"You want me to write a poem?"

"I am leaving pen and paper with you. Just write a new poem and we'll be done."

"A poem?"

"Yes, a poem of progress. A poem that guides your readers back to the right path. It needn't be a long one. A short poem will do very well. I am leaving pen and paper here. They'll serve you dinner shortly. I am not going to disturb you any more tonight. I'll come back in the morning for the poem. Bye."

10

A poem?

He has never dreamed of writing a poem. How does one begin?

Saleha's face appears before him.

"*Saleha? Is that you?*"

"*Weren't you in love with me once?*"

"*Yes.*"

"*Did you love me a lot?*"

"*Yes a lot.*"

"*Then why didn't you tell me so?*"

"*I never understood my own feelings, Saleha.*"

"And now?"

"Now it would be wrong of me to think such thoughts. I am married to someone else and it's improper to tell you that I loved you."

"Don't you love your homeland?"

"Yes."

"But it's no longer yours."

"What do you mean?"

"Somebody has wrested your homeland away from you."

"So what?"

"Do you still love it?"

"Yes."

"Isn't that wrong?"

"No Saleha, it is at moments such as these that one truly loves one's country. Let me tell you something funny. I was born in Burdwan, not East Bengal. Even after I came to Dacca I never thought of East Bengal or Bangladesh as my homeland. Home would always remind me of Burdwan."

"And now?"

"That's what I am telling you. When bullets rained over the city and tanks rolled across it, when houses were demolished and corpses piled up on the streets I saw them raising their own flags from the roofs of buildings and tearing down ours. I wanted to scream silently in despair. It was the same way I had felt when I received the invitation card to your wedding."

"Did you weep?"

"No I didn't weep. Not then and not now. When something hits you this way you can't express your sorrow any more. Your entire being is transformed into a silent wall of tears. But strangely enough it was then that I found my heart filling with love for Bangladesh. That love has sustained me through everything that has happened to me since then."

"Do you still love me?"

"Yes, I do. I love you and everybody else. I can love anybody now. Are you all right Saleha? Are you well?"

"Do you love me?"

"Yes."

"Will you write a poem for me, Nazrul?"

"A poem?"

"Yes a poem, about me. For me."

"I can't write poetry, Saleha."

"You can."

"No I can't. I don't know how poetry gets written."

"You do. Look deep inside you and you will find a poem inscribed."

"No, Saleha."

"It is there, Nazrul."

"No, nothing's there."

"But there is. I can see it. Just get up once and look inside your heart. You will find it written in letters of gold. Read that poem, Nazrul. Read it out to me."

Nazrul scrambles to his feet, muttering, "*Saleha! Saleha!*"

A khaki hears him and comes into the room. Nazrul's blood turns to ice when he sees the soldier. He collapses on the bed and asks for some water. The khaki promises to get him some soon and leaves, slamming the door behind him.

The piece of paper on the table next to his bed, held in place by the pen, rustles as if it too wants to fly away like a bird. Nazrul stares at the blank emptiness of the paper for a while. He is no longer worried about the passage of time and is oblivious to whether a lifetime passes him by or not, before the sympathetic man reappears and asks him in a friendly tone whether he has written the poem.

"No."

"It's no easy business, writing a poem. But you must try."

"You are making a mistake."

"Maybe. I know that one can't force oneself to write poetry."

"Then why am I being forced?"

"Because we desperately need a new poem from you. I have kept all the newspapers informed. If you can finish the poem by tonight, it will be printed in bold letters in all the newspapers tomorrow morning. Everyone's waiting. Ok, let me come back after an hour. Have you eaten something?"

"What?"

Nazrul is startled by this inquiry. No one here has asked him such a question before. But the moment he thinks of food, his stomach begins to churn viciously and his mouth fills with bile. He is forced to slap his hands to his mouth.

"I'll come back later for the poem," the man says as he leaves the room.

Nazrul lies supine, his eyes closed. The paper placed near his head flutters like wings. Kumkum leans against the empty whiteness of the wall and weeps.

"*Why do you cry? Stop crying, will you?*"

Kumkum makes no reply and continues to shed tears. Nazrul gets incensed and says, "*Don't you know that too much crying fetches bad luck? Shut up, Kumkum, just shut up.*"

Khokon comes tripping into the room and rushes into his lap. "*Abbu, do you know I won the first prize in recitation today!*"

"*Where?*"

"*At school of course. It was the last day before summer vacation. There was an assembly and I read out a poem. Do you know which one?*"

"*No. Which one?*"

"*A funny rhyme.*"

"*Read it out to me.*"

Khokon jumps off his lap and stands in the middle of the room, making various gestures as he recites the poem.

Near Habu's duck pond was I found
Running for life from Babu's pet hound,
Telling the beast to stop
As it chased me round and round!

The rhyme courses through every part of Nazrul's brain—*Near Habu's duck pond was I found, running for life from Babu's pet hound . . .*

What made a poem? Words after words, rhymes following rhymes, stanzas after stanzas? But what made the subject of a poem? What could one write a poem about?

The door opens and the man reappears. He asks if the poem is done.

Nazrul gives him a burning look from his deep-set eyes, set in their skeletal sockets. The man looks shamefaced and hurriedly shuts the door.

One poem is all it will take for his name to be splashed on the newspapers the next day.

Telling the beast to stop, as it chased me round and round . . .

Nazrul circles his bed on all fours, unable to stand up. He drags his legs around the bed like a wounded carnivore, hunting ceaselessly for a moonlit pool of water in the darkness of a deep forest. A fire begins to burn inside his head, its flames licking the cells of his brain and filling them with the arcane words of an ancient Persian prayer. Sailen Babu, his history professor in college, appears before him, waving his hands dramatically and lecturing, Zarathushtra spread the light of a new truth among the ancient Persians; he said that there were two gods, Ormuzd the god of good and Ahriman the god of evil, and the two fought incessantly in heaven. Sometimes one claimed victory and sometimes the other.

Nazrul comes to a halt and emits a deep groan. He resumes circling the bed on all fours. Suddenly, for the first time the visage of the mad poet Nazrul Islam comes before his eyes, with his curly tresses, sturdy shoulders and dark eyes, a silent smile playing at the corner of his lip. The two of them stare at each other, two men with the same name but different identities, across a bridge that spans a bottomless abyss to join them together, each letter of their shared name engraved on each of its girders.

11

The same man comes back, helps Nazrul off the floor and lowers him on to the bed. This time Nazrul is conscious and stares at the man with a tranquil gaze.

"The poem?"

A silent smile plays at the corner of Nazrul's lip.

"You haven't written it?"

The smile brightens.

"Don't you know the trouble you are bringing upon your head?"

"I know."

"You do? But still you refuse to write?"

"Yes."

"Just one poem?"

"I won't write a single poem."

"But you will be free if you do."

"Of what?"

"Your captivity."

"I am not a captive."

"You are making a terrible mistake."

"No. You are."

"The moment you write the poem you can go."

"Go where?"

"Jafarganj."

"Where is that?"

"Don't you know where Jafarganj is?"

"I know where Jafarganj is. It is in my country. And I am in my country. My country is called Bangladesh."

A hard slap falls across his face. The room fills up silently with khaki-clad men.

"Won't you write the poem?" He is asked one more time.

"No."

"Then what poem do you wish to write? A poem of protest?"

"If possible, I would have written one."

"But you can't write poetry, can you?"

"I am not sure."

"You're still lying, aren't you?"

"I don't lie."

"Never?"

"Never."

"Haven't you incited the populace to rebellion?"

"You are better informed than I am."

"Haven't you urged the Bengalis to take up arms?"

"Ask the Bengalis that."

"You still mean to say that you are not the poet Kazi Nazrul Islam?"

"You are saying that I am."

He is knocked down to the floor and his kneecap broken with a short, stout stick. Strangely enough he feels no pain and the dull crack of the kneecap breaking seems to come from somewhere else altogether.

"Do you deny that you are Nazrul?"

"I am Nazrul."

"Nazrul, the poet?"

"I want to be a poet."

"Don't you want to write poetry?"

"Not for you. No."

The short stick comes down like lightning on his other kneecap and shatters it.

"Are you a poet now?"

"Yes, I am."

"Won't you write a poem?"

"No, I refuse."

Somebody kicks him on his stomach and he falls to the floor on his belly. A sharp pain courses through his hip. The hip rises once to fall back upon the floor. Somebody straightens him with another kick.

"Nazrul, will you write?"

"No."

His left elbow is now broken at the joint. He silently screams at Kumkum, urging her to leave. Take Khokon and Mamata with you, he tells her, far, far away from this stinking hell filled with water.

"Think again, Nazrul."

"I have thought."

"Your right hand is still left undamaged. You can still write a poem should you choose to."

"I know."

"Will you write?"

"No. I won't."

His right elbow too is broken at the joint. Blood fills his mouth as a boot presses down on his chest and in his thirst he tries to lick some of it with his tongue. But his tongue is numb, merely filling up his mouth like an immobile object. Tufts of his hair are pulled up and come off in the hands of his torturers. Soon the room is filled with hair, floating about like pollen from the *nagkesar* tree.

He is taken out of the room and his body cast into an open area next to a plantain grove. The men proceed to dig a hole in the ground.

Nazrul tries to grasp at the clods of earth with his fingers. But his fingers refuse to secure a grip and grow still. The shrubs at eye-level remain mute, like dear friends come to pay him a last visit. The smell of damp earth wafts across his spirit. From the corner of his eye he can spy the hole being dug and the clods of earth being pulled out with a spade, spreading the damp smell all around.

He hears the faint crack of his spine snapping and his chest feels very warm. He can hear a jackal howling far away.

Without ever having written a single poem, he, the poet Kazi Nazrul Islam, is kicked into the hole for having refused to write one last poem.

His eyes stay open till the very end.

Forbidden Incense

1

The train chugged into Nabagram and came to a halt. Only one more station between Nabagram and Jaleswari—the end of the line and Bilkis's destination. She had reached Torsa Junction from Dacca at eleven o'clock and managed to get onto the Jaleswari-bound train only at three. Usually the connecting train was available immediately, but these days no train ran on time, nor was expected to.

Normally the train from Torsa to Jaleswari ran slowly. When she was a child Bilkis had learned from her father that the tracks had been laid over the old District Board highway. The foundations were thus not very sturdy and there were numerous bends to negotiate. That was the reason trains ran slowly over this segment, to avoid getting derailed. Still, the distance between Torsa and Jaleswari was normally covered in an hour. On this occasion, however, the train had taken nearly two hours to reach Nabagram.

Ever since she had boarded the train, Bilkis had been aware of strange whispers circulating among the passengers. She had attributed this to the reticence that normally overcame villagers in the uncommon presence of a city-bred woman like her. Also times were such that most people spoke in low voices in public, fearing to completely trust even those they knew well, let alone strangers.

Though Bilkis had never seen it halt for more than two minutes at Nabagram, this time the stipulated two minutes passed without the train showing any sign of moving. Most of the passengers got off quickly and silently when the train came to a halt, disappearing within minutes down the narrow track that ran through the wild shrubbery beyond the station. The rest of the passengers, those bound for Jaleswari like her, sat for some time before they too scattered like animals dispersed by stones. Within a few minutes the whole train was empty except for her.

Bilkis peered out of the window but was unable to fathom what was going on. Silence prevailed all around her, other than the steamy wheeze of the aged engine. Her watch told her it was ten past five, and she decided to get off the train with her small suitcase. She had specifically chosen it before leaving Dacca so that she could carry it herself, without depending on the mercy of porters. Spotting the guard marching off towards the station building, she caught up with him. "I want to go to Jaleswari," she told him.

The guard stared at her with a bewildered, uncomprehending look— almost as though he had never heard the name Jaleswari. Or maybe as though he found it difficult to fit a smart woman like Bilkis into the sunlit, rural environs of Nabagram, and was not sure whether she was an illusion. Times were such that people witnessed nearly anything and everything, yet found it difficult to let go of their native sense of wonder and incredulity.

"Will this train go to Jaleswari?" Bilkis asked him again, anxiously.

The guard stared at her some more, unnecessarily exchanging the red and green flags between his hands. Then without saying anything and muttering something unintelligible he disappeared under the thatched roof of the station house.

Bilkis looked around and found no one she could direct her question to. Though she had traveled from Dacca to Jaleswari numerous times since she was young, crossing Nabagram on the way, this was the first time that she had actually got off here. She had no idea what lay beyond the shrubbery behind the station house or who lived here. For a moment she felt helpless and lost. Then her eyes fell upon a young boy not older than seventeen or eighteen, sitting next to a well just outside the station and staring at her. The moment their eyes met the boy moved his own away and vanished. Bilkis had hoped she could have at least had a word with him even if he was unable to help her about her journey to Jaleswari. With not a soul around, she felt so alone and afraid that it was easy to mistake even the rustling of the trees and bushes behind her for the murmurs of an unknown conspiracy.

She decided to go into the station house. The man seated behind a table, clearly the stationmaster, looked startled and unsettled by her entry. The guard, who had also been seated at the table with his head cradled in his hands, looked up at her, giving her the same uncomprehending stare as before.

"I want to go to Jaleswari."

The stationmaster gave Bilkis a vacant look and asked, "Where are you coming from?"

"From Dacca."

"Are trains running that side?"

"Yes they are. I am here, am I not?"

The stationmaster exchanged glances with the guard. Just then the engine driver arrived. "What's the news Master Sahib?" he asked.

"What news? No news. Return to Torsa. This train won't go any further."

"They could have told me earlier." The driver grumbled. "I could have simply backed the engine up to Nabagram and gone straight back. The stationmaster at Torsa told me nothing."

"What's the problem with backing up now?" The guard asked in a querulous tone.

"Well, you are not the one who has to take a three-mile detour to reverse the engine at Torsa, are you? Do you know what's going on there? Anything can happen at any time and I certainly don't want to be caught up in any of it."

Bilkis had been listening with increasing trepidation to the conversation, hanging on every word in order to extract some more information. Now she cut in and asked, "So the train won't go to Jaleswari at all?"

The three men looked at her silently. Finally the stationmaster said, "No."

"Why not?"

Her question was met with silence.

"Why won't the train go?" She persisted.

Without replying, the stationmaster turned to the guard, saying, "Don't delay any more. I have orders to send the train back the moment it came. You don't want to be caught in the dark on the return journey, do you?"

The guard exchanged a quick and meaningful look with the stationmaster, and then, without further ado, picked up the two flags and headed for the train. The engine driver did not stir immediately, maybe because he wanted to express some more displeasure. But the stationmaster told him not to waste time bickering over trifles, and he too made his exit. The stationmaster got up and followed the driver to the door, where he stood, craning his neck to see the train depart.

Bilkis waited, unsure of what to do. For a minute she considered getting on the train and returning. But she knew very well that going on to Jaleswari was the only option for her and dropped that thought. Suddenly her eyes fell upon a face framed in the station house window—the boy she had seen earlier. The moment he saw her looking at him, he moved away.

The engine emitted a long hiss and its wheels began to turn. From the station house Bilkis saw the bogies move past her, followed by the engine, which was pushing the carriages. The stationmaster, who had perhaps forgotten her, turned and looked visibly surprised to see her seated in the uncertain light which penetrated through the small window of the room.

"You are coming from Dacca?"

"Yes."

"Why do you want to go to Jaleswari?"

"It's important."

The stationmaster slumped into his chair with a worried look, threw up his hands and said, "There's nothing I can do." Then, perhaps because it struck him that it would be unfair to be so brusque with a woman so clearly in distress, he asked sympathetically, "Do you have someone living in Jaleswari?"

"Yes, my mother. And my brother, who studies at Rangpur College. Then there's my widowed sister with her two children. What's happened at Jaleswari?" Having talked about herself, Bilkis finally asked the question which had been weighing her down.

Without replying directly the stationmaster asked, "But how will you get there now? It is five miles to Jaleswari from here."

Bilkis had a sudden vision of Jaleswari going up in flames, tongues of fire licking the houses and reducing them to charred ruins that stood silently once the fire went out, amidst a gaping silence that enveloped the town. She scrambled to her feet and asked in a worried voice, "Is it possible to reach Jaleswari?"

The stationmaster pondered over her question for a bit before answering, "I can't say for sure."

"What have you heard?"

"What I have heard is not good."

"What isn't good?" A note of deep concern for her brother, sister and mother lay in Bilkis's question. For a moment she gave up hope of seeing them again, just as she had given up hope of seeing her husband Altaf ever again.

"Things were all right so far," the stationmaster said. "There was no trouble."

"That's what I heard too. My mother wrote to me last Wednesday."

The stationmaster looked at her doubtfully, not sure how frank he could be with a stranger. If Bilkis had been a man maybe he would have sent him packing by now. But he hesitated, not least because the prospect of having a conversation with a smartly turned out city woman at a time when he could easily slip through the cracks of terror-stricken events and disappear was not entirely without its appeal.

"The last three months had been quiet around here," he said. "After the incident in Dacca in March, the military came from Rangpur in the first month of April."

"My brother wrote to me that people were leaving Jaleswari then."

"Not just Jaleswari, many people left this place as well and crossed to the far bank of the Adhkosha for fear of the military and the rioting, Urdu-speaking Biharis. But the army declared that those who did not return would have their houses razed. That's when many people who had left went back. Since then things have been quiet for the past few months. There were rumors that those who had fled to India would return to take up arms, but nothing like that happened. But this morning I heard that the railway bridge across the canal from Jaleswari which meets the Adhkosha has been destroyed with dynamite. People say that the army has been firing in Jaleswari."

"Is the army stationed there?"

"They set up a camp last month."

"What about the people in Jaleswari?"

"Nobody can say."

Bilkis felt cold, clammy fingers of fear gripping her chest. She remembered Altaf, but, after his absence for the past few months, more as a thought than a real person. Was she fated not to see the rest of her family too? She gripped the suitcase in her hand and stood up. The stationmaster raised his hand briefly as if to desist her, but then thought better of it.

"What will you do now?"

"I'll go to Jaleswari."

"You have to walk five miles."

"I have to go."

"Will you walk all this distance?" The stationmaster sounded both worried and curious.

"Let me see."

"But alone . . . "

Bilkis thought it over and replied, "What can I do?"

"Normally I could have sent someone to accompany you but these days, nobody wants to go there, especially not with the night coming on."

"I can go."

Bilkis stood on the platform and looked ahead where the tracks disappeared round a bend into the trees. The daylight was still bright and she could see a white cow straddling the tracks and munching peacefully. A sliver of grey cloud hung in the sky like a puff of smoke from gunfire.

Bilkis took the narrow footpath that ran alongside the rail tracks and headed towards Jaleswari.

2

Soon she suspected that she was being followed. Once, she stopped abruptly, her ears ready to catch any suspicious sound. But except for a few chirping birds, the rustle of wind through the trees and a sudden crack echoing in a bamboo grove she heard nothing. She proceeded on her way, turning a corner that removed the station house from her line of sight. In front of her lay a large shed and miles of open fields with the rail tracks stretching to the horizon. Suddenly Bilkis felt part of a vastness that made her weak and tired. But she continued to walk. From time to time everything clouded over and she could only see the faces of her mother, brother and sister against the background of their long, tin-roofed house with a mango tree behind it. The tree was normally visible from a distance and Bilkis found it comforting to set her bearings by the tall, imagined tree and move forward with determination.

This time there was no mistaking the sound. Bilkis turned around and spotted the boy she had seen earlier, running towards her over the sleepers of the railway lines. As she turned towards him the boy halted uncertainly, neither advancing nor going back. For a moment he seemed to be a part of the landscape itself. He took a few steps forward and then stopped again.

Bilkis felt the surge of a mild curiosity and signaled to the boy to come forward, taking a few steps towards him herself. They came to a halt with a gap of about ten feet between them.

"Hey, what do you want? What's your name?"

The boy appeared younger than her own brother and Bilkis had no problem addressing him in a familiar tone. Also, she felt irritated that the boy had been following her since she had got off the train.

Instead of replying, the boy looked her up and down.

"Why are you following me?" Although she felt uncomfortable, Bilkis could not attribute her discomfort solely to fear. In fact, it was the boy who looked a bit afraid, though she had no idea of what. "Come over here," she told him.

The boy came forward and spoke for the first time. "Are you coming from Dacca?" he asked.

"Yes."

"Do you want to go to Jaleswari?"

"That's the idea."

"Please don't go!" The boy put on a pleading, fearful tone.

"Why not?"

"You are all by yourself."

"What can I do? The train went back as you saw."

"Why don't you go later?"

"I have to go now."

"Please don't." This time the boy spoke with a conviction that Bilkis found difficult to ignore.

Perhaps he knew more about the goings-on at Jaleswari than the stationmaster did, she thought. "Why do you say that?" she asked. "Is the situation very bad there?"

"No worse than usual. People have been coming and going."

"Do you know anything of what happened this morning?"

"Not very well. But you shouldn't go alone like this."

"Won't I reach before it gets dark?"

"Maybe, if you walk quickly."

Bilkis was touched by his candor and concern for her. She gave him a kind look and said, "Then I'd better be on my way."

The boy began to walk with her. Bilkis assumed that he would go back after a while and thought no more of him. The journey of five miles which lay ahead occupied her mind. She could not remember when she had last traveled such a long distance on foot.

"I had a sister like you," the boy suddenly said.

Bilkis noted the past tense in his words and stopped, waiting to hear the rest of what had to be a sad story. But the boy spoke no more and continued to walk silently beside her. They went past fields devoid of any sign of human habitation, though these were times when the local inhabitants thought it better to hide themselves from view. There was no one resting in the shade of the tall *jamun* tree they passed and not even a domestic animal was in sight. Tall reeds bent over the green, stagnant water of a nearby pond, quivering gently in the breeze. Suddenly the cawing of a flying crow broke the stillness momentarily.

Bilkis felt secretly grateful that the boy was accompanying her and the need to build a bridge with him to induce him to walk further with her. Keeping the boy's sister in mind she asked, "Did the military . . . "

"Yes, they killed her. Finally."

Finally? After what? Bilkis felt a shiver run through her spine as the thought crossed her mind. The boy quietly took her suitcase from her and said, "So you are determined to go?"

"How can I go back after coming all the way from Dacca?"

"That's right, of course."

"Where was your sister?"

"At Jaleswari."

"Was she married?"

"She was supposed to get married. All arrangements had been made. Then this happened."

Bilkis could not understand how the boy could be from Nabagram and yet have an unmarried sister living in Jaleswari. Where was he from really—Jaleswari or Nabagram? As if he had heard her question before she could say it out loud, the boy said,

"The Biharis killed my parents and younger brother one night during the rioting. I would have fled to India but could not pluck up the courage to go on my own. A friend of mine brought me to Nabagram from Jaleswari."

Bilkis realized the boy was from Jaleswari. She was also intrigued that he had trusted a stranger enough to tell her about his plans to flee to India. By then the two of them had traveled a fair distance and a thicket of trees pressed close to the rail tracks, their path visible through a tunnel under the overhanging branches.

"How much further will you come with me?" Bilkis asked the boy.

"Let's see."

"Aren't you afraid?"

"Of what?"

"I believe the army opened fire in Jaleswari today. What if they grab you?"

"At least I know my way around here. You don't even know that."

"Why do you want to take such a risk for me?"

The boy gave no reply. He looked embarrassed all of a sudden.

"It's better that you turn back."

"If we are together there's nothing to fear."

"But how will you get back to Nabagram? Won't it get too late?"

"If you let me sleep in your house for the night, I'll be fine."

"Do you know my house?"

"Of course I do!" The boy said enthusiastically. "You are Kader Master's . . . "

"Did you know my father?"

"I have seen him, though I don't remember him too well. He died the year I went from minor to high school, you see. Otherwise he would have taught us English. Everyone used to say how there was no better a teacher of English than him."

The two of them entered the cool, leafy tunnel, the leaves of trees wet and shiny around them. The footpath disappeared and they were forced to come on to the rail tracks.

"Where is your house in Jaleswari?" Bilkis asked and wished she had not. It was cruel to remind the boy of the home and family he had lost.

The boy hesitated and then replied, "Behind the post office on the far shore of the marshland."

Bilkis decided not to press her inquiries any further, though thoughts of the dead family of her chance-found companion kept hovering in her head.

Her thoughts veered naturally to Altaf. Was he still alive? On the night of the twenty-fifth of March the army had set fire to the office of the newspaper where Altaf worked. Altaf had gone for the night shift and never returned. Neither of the two corpses retrieved from the flames could be firmly identified as his. Shamsher, a journalist friend of Altaf's with another paper had told her several times: "*Bhabi*, I am sure Altaf is alive."

But if he was alive why didn't Altaf return? Every night Bilkis would hold the radio surreptitiously to her ear and listen to the broadcasts from the Free Bengal radio station, expecting, maybe, to hear Altaf 's voice on it soon. But she heard nothing, though Shamsher had told her, "*Bhabi*, Altaf has escaped to India and it's not easy to send word from there. But he will surely slip some news across the border and you will know that he is fine. Just a matter of time."

"You didn't tell me your name," Bilkis remarked.

"My name? My name is Siraj."

"Siraj?"

The boy suddenly looked tense and distracted though Bilkis could not fathom why. Had he sensed something that she had not? Were the military hiding in the surrounding forest, waiting to pounce upon them? She drew closer to him and asked, "Siraj, how far have we come?"

"We still have a long way to go."

"A long way? Still?"

"We haven't walked much."

"Must be two miles."

Siraj laughed out and said, "How can you say that, *Didi*?" then grew alert again and whispered, "Let's push on before it gets dark."

The two of them came back on to the open fields. "If you could walk on the sleepers we'd go faster," Siraj observed. But Bilkis was not happy about tripping across sleepers in her sari and they had to walk by the side of the tracks.

"If only we could have got hold of a bullock cart." Siraj said, "I spoke to a couple of fellows when you were with the station-master, but after the bridge to Jaleswari was destroyed today, nobody wants to venture to that side."

Bilkis was surprised at the pains the boy had taken on her behalf, unknown to her. She knew of her father's students who still remembered him fondly, but Siraj, even without having actually studied under him seemed to have decided to go out of his way for his daughter. Her heart swelled with pride for her dead father and her mother's face rose before her eyes. Her mother would often grumble that her father had never made it beyond the position of assistant headmaster of the high school. "So what, I have my students, don't I?" her father would retort.

Was her family all right after the incident at Jaleswari in the morning? Bilkis began to feel distraught.

"It's getting late."

Bilkis placed her foot on a sleeper, bunched the sari in her hand to draw up the hem and leaped gingerly on to the next one. She stumbled once or twice at first but her body soon adjusted to the rhythm of the movement as she advanced, taking one stride after another.

"How much longer do we have to go Siraj?"

"You must be getting tired. Should we stop for a while?"

"No, no, we'll be late. I have to get home Siraj, I can't rest till I am there."

"Nobody will harm the master's family or his residence."

"Then you don't know what happened at Dacca. They dragged university professors from their homes and shot them dead. The Hindu professors—they first tortured with bayonets and then killed."

Siraj trembled.

"Have you really not heard?"

Siraj gave her a wan smile and a fearful look.

"How much further? Tell me."

"About two miles."

"It's time you went back Siraj. I am now worried about you. The military targets boys of your age. There are stories of bodies floating down the river, their hands and legs tied, the blood sucked from their veins with needles—all boys of your age. Please go back. I can continue on my own from here."

Siraj halted briefly and seemed to mull over her request in his head. His face betrayed no emotion and he stood still as a statue. Then, having apparently resolved the debate in favor of not going back, he began to walk with her again, silently.

"You are a strange fellow!" Bilkis exclaimed.

Siraj gave no reply.

3

They reached Jaleswari as evening set in. Though the limits of the town were considered to begin from the *Dak* Bungalow, which stood at the crossing of three roads, they were unable to take this route because of the blown-up bridge, which they had to circumvent by passing through the woods and the town cemetery, a route which saw them coming back on to the rail tracks adjoining the distant signal for Jaleswari station.

An eerie silence reigned all around them. From a distance the houses looked dark and empty. The silence here was different from the silence of the open fields—an urban silence that gave away the presence of human beings, who dared not make any noise—a silence filled with the possibility of sound but strangely bereft of any.

Bilkis threw an anxious glance at Siraj who remained quiet and sullen.

The shortest way to reach Bilkis's house followed the rail tracks and they took this route, alert to the slightest movement but unable to see or hear anything unusual. They walked briskly till they came upon a path that crossed the rail tracks at a distance of a few paces from the house of Kader Master to the left. Even in the dark one could spy the long, tin-roofed building with the mango tree behind it.

Bilkis nearly ran the last few steps to her house and went up to the doors. Siraj followed her and remarked, "The house appears to be empty."

Bilkis had realized as much the moment she had noticed the gaping open doors revealing the congealed darkness inside. The two of them lost no time scurrying in because it was safer inside than out in the open. Even in the darkness they could spot clothes hanging from a line, a bucket full of water in a corner, cooking utensils lying on the kitchen floor as if somebody had just finished a meal, a black-and-white chequered football rolling indolently on the porch. The armchair Kader Master was fond of reclining in stood outside the bedroom, somehow heightening the sense of emptiness which pervaded the house.

Bilkis searched all the rooms and came back to lean her arms on the back of the chair. "Where's everybody?" she whispered.

"I can't tell. The neighboring houses are silent too."

"What are we going to do now, Siraj?"

"Please sit down for a while."

When Bilkis continued to stand there with her hands on the backrest of the chair, Siraj repeated, "Please sit. You've walked a long way." He literally forced her to sit in the chair. Siraj looked different now from the adolescent youth of the afternoon, as if he had traversed not just many miles but also many years during the journey. His voice appeared firmer, his actions more assured than before.

"Sit and rest. Don't upset yourself." Siraj went and surveyed the house once on his own, looking into each room. He went out through the main door and returned after a few minutes. Bilkis clasped his hands in anxiety for news.

"The neighbors are all gone. They must have fled."

But what if they had met a worse fate? The worry that maybe they had been butchered en masse showed in Bilkis's eyes and she could no longer sit still. "What then?" she asked.

"*Apa*, please sit." Siraj forced her back into the chair and thought for a minute. "Do you think you can stay here alone for a while? Halfan-hour or so?" he asked.

"Where do you plan to go?"

"To see if I can get some news of what happened."

"No, don't go anywhere." Bilkis grabbed his hand and pleaded.

"Nothing will happen to me, don't worry."

"But is there anyone to give you information?"

"There are some shops and houses near the station. Maybe I can find someone there."

"What if you get caught on the way? Don't be foolhardy, please!"

Siraj smiled and said. "*Didi* you don't know anything. The military rarely venture out at night. All their work takes place in daylight."

Bilkis let go of his hand. "Can you be here on your own?

"I won't be long." Siraj repeated. When she nodded he went out but came back. "Do you want to sit here in the porch?"

"Why? What's the problem?"

"Anybody standing at the main door will see you. I don't want to shut the door to avoid raising any suspicion. Why don't you wait near the kitchen? But don't make a sound till you hear my voice, not even if you hear a noise. I'll come and call."

Siraj melted into the darkness with quick steps. The moment he left Bilkis felt the darkness around her crowd in. She went near the well next to the kitchen but felt even more afraid and moved away quickly.

The porch of the neighboring house could be seen on the other side of the fence running past the kitchen. Her mother would often part the fencing to speak to the woman who lived next door, whose husband owned a cycle-repair shop and suffered from asthma. Sometimes his attacks were so bad that all of them, including Bilkis, would stay up most of the night listening to his wheezy, troubled breathing.

The house now lay silent. Bilkis parted the fencing but saw nothing but darkness ahead of her. She craned her neck to sense any sign of a human presence but found none.

Suddenly she had the feeling that someone was standing at the kitchen door. She spun around quickly but saw no one. Though nobody could have escaped unseen, she still ran out of the room to the porch. She touched the clothes and found them all dry and stiff—a shirt, a few clothes belonging to the children, a towel and a pair of white saris. The folds of the saris swelled up from time to time in the gentle breeze and then subsided back to hang like mournful banners. Bilkis clutched one end of a sari and pressed it to her face. Strange, how the smell of the wearer had not completely left the sari even after it had been washed. Without quite knowing how, she began to feel the presence of her mother and sister around the empty house.

Were they dead? In which case, what happened to their bodies? Were there telltale bloodstains on the floor that she had missed in the dark? Should she light a lamp? If she headed back to the kitchen she knew that she would be sure to find a lantern on a familiar shelf, matchbox next to it. Bilkis went back to the kitchen and with practiced movements reached the familiar shelf. Her fingers searched and touched not one but two kerosene lamps and a matchbox next to them. She removed a lamp cautiously. Siraj had warned her not to give out any sign that the house was inhabited. She ran a real risk of doing that if she lit a lamp now. But then she told herself that since the military did not venture out at night, she would remain undiscovered. Bilkis struck a match and looked around before lighting the wick and turning it down to lower the flame. Even in the uncertain lamplight her eyes made out a large *korai* kept on the stove. The inhabitants of the house had had to leave even before finishing their meal. In a corner lay a sieve with grains of rice that were being sifted, still on it. A plate lay on the porch with a couple of *rotis* and a half-eaten banana on it.

Shielding the flame, Bilkis walked quickly into the bedroom. Strangely she no longer felt afraid. It was a moment when she somehow felt herself rising above the reality of the situation. When she entered the bedroom she searched the floor for bloodstains and then went on to explore the bed, the walls and the small adjoining room that belonged to her brother. Where was Khoka? Had he been at Rangpur or home? The bed looked like it had been slept in. Maybe Khoka never got a chance to go back to Rangpur and was here at Jaleswari. Her heart quaked a little as she thought of Khoka and the fate that could have befallen him. Didn't the military pick out boys of his age for slaughter?

She realized that she had forgotten all about Siraj and came out to the porch, feeling perturbed. He seemed to have gone for ever. What had happened to her family? Where had they gone and when? What had made them leave in such a hurry? There was no visible sign of a struggle anywhere and it did not appear that they had been killed. Had they sought refuge on the far bank of the river as they had done earlier?

Bilkis put the lamp out and dragged the armchair to one corner, trying not to make any noise. From where she now sat the front door was no longer visible. For the first time her legs began to ache terribly from the rigors of the five-mile walk. Gradually the ache spread from her legs to her back. Hunger and thirst coiled up together to raise a fresh ache inside her stomach. The inside of her head felt empty, horribly empty.

When Altaf had disappeared she had not hoped that he would ever come back. But, against all hope, she could not resist her expectation of some news of him—even a surreptitious midnight knock with Altaf standing outside the door. Soon her savings ran out and two months of rent fell due. The landlord was unrecognizable these days with the beard he sported and the cap he wore. He would visit her and, besides pressuring her for the rent, would offer unsolicited advice: "Go to your family in the country, it's unsafe to live around here . . . "

Next, Shamsher would come and tell her: "*Bhabi*, haven't you heard that trouble has erupted in Dacca? Didn't you hear the sound of firing day before yesterday near Farmgate? Our boys had attacked . . . "

Shamsher feared that the army would now be on the alert to ferret out houses with a secret link to India. If Altaf had really fled to India then they would be sure to arrest Bilkis soon.

"I think it is best for you to join your family in the village, *Bhabi* . . . "

Had Altaf really fled to India and joined the liberation forces? Every time Bilkis heard of how those boys had blown up a bridge, cast grenades or finished off a truckload of soldiers, she would wonder if Altaf was involved in any of those heroic acts. What about the shots she heard being fired nightly in Dacca? Were they all fired by the military? Was Altaf 's finger not on even one of the triggers pulled? Her heart would beat with the double trepidation that came with wishing for Altaf 's wellbeing on the one hand and pride in the resistance that was taking shape against the regime on the other.

Sometimes she thought of how she would possibly have had a child in her arms by now if they had desisted from family planning last year. Altaf 's child. Hurt welled up inside her at the thought. After five years of marriage they should really have thought of raising a family. But then she thought of how a child would only have added to the mounting problems in times such as these and was grateful for being childless.

What if Altaf really never came back? What if he had died the same night he disappeared? Or what if he was silent on purpose?

Had he fallen out of love with her? Had she not loved him enough not to deserve that?

"*Apa*."

Bilkis jumped to her feet with a start, not sure if she had indeed heard a voice, or if her imagination had played a trick on her.

Siraj emerged from the darkness. "It's me, *Apa*." He looked around quickly and asked, "Was anybody here?"

"No. I was ok. Did you hear anything?"

"Hmm."

"What?"

"The bridge across the canal isn't destroyed completely. The rails on one side are gone though."

Bilkis was more interested in news of her family than in the bridge but feared to ask a direct question. She looked at Siraj with anxious inquiry in her eyes. A sliver of light from somewhere fell on his eyes, making them look unnaturally bright, almost glistening with tears.

"From what I heard, your family is safe." Siraj said.

"Whom did you hear from? Where are they?"

"Most people living on this side of town managed to make their way across the river this afternoon. Your family was spotted among the people who went. Unfortunately not many people on the side where the Biharis are a majority could cross over. The military has armed the Biharis with guns, you see."

Siraj spoke without drawing breath, almost as if it were a rehearsed speech. Bilkis noticed that he seemed relieved when he had finished. She concluded that his voice sounded different because of the excitement of being out under dangerous circumstances.

"What have you been doing? I got delayed."

"Sitting by myself."

"Weren't you afraid?"

Bilkis shook her head briefly. The feeling of fear seemed suddenly alien to her. "Are you sure they made their way across the river?" She asked Siraj again.

"Yes, a few volunteers in the neighborhood knocked on every door and helped escort the women up to the river bank."

Bilkis felt disturbed at the mention of only women and asked, "And what about Khoka?"

"Your brother?"

"Yes, didn't Khoka go with them?"

"Yes, everyone has made it to the far side, don't worry. Let the night end. Tomorrow morning I'll try to take you across the river too."

"But didn't you say that it was easier to avoid the military at night? Won't it be more difficult to cross during the day?"

"We'll dress you in tattered clothes and disguise you as a farmer's wife."

Bilkis grasped his hand and said, "You've done a lot for me, my brother." Somewhere in Siraj's face she thought she saw a hint of Khoka. It was strange how two faces could blend into one at emotional moments such as this.

"You haven't eaten, have you?" Siraj said quickly.

"I am not hungry. You?"

"*Didi*, *Apa*, how can you starve all night? Isn't there anything in the kitchen?"

"Let me light a lamp and see."

"No. For heaven's sake don't do that!"

Bilkis remembered having lit a lamp a while ago and her heart skipped a beat.

"Actually it's not wise for us to be here anymore."

"Why not?"

"The Biharis know that the houses here are deserted and they might come to plunder. They are the ones ruling the roost around here now."

"Then?"

"Let's see if we can find some *muri* or something in the kitchen. Then we can be on our way."

"But where shall we go?"

"Anywhere but here, *Apa*. It's dangerous to stay here tonight, I've heard." Bilkis heard the quaver in Siraj's voice. "Don't be afraid," she said, trying to give him strength, strength she tapped into from deep within herself, "I have stayed alone in a house in Dacca for months."

"But we have to leave this place soon."

"We will. Let me light a lamp and check the kitchen first. Don't worry, I lit one before you came."

4

They found nothing in the kitchen but some uncooked rice. "Let's forget it, they must have taken whatever they had when they left." Siraj appeared to be in a hurry.

"Yes, they had children with them." The faces of the two children of her widowed sister swam before Bilkis's eyes.

"Do you want to check inside the rooms?"

"For what?"

"In case they left something valuable, which we can take with us?"

"What is there to take with us, Siraj?"

Siraj blew the lamp out.

"You've eaten nothing all day," Bilkis remarked.

"Neither have you, *Apa*."

The two of them left the house silently. Once they came up to the road, Siraj looked up and down it but noticed nothing suspicious. "There doesn't seem to be anyone here," he whispered, "but it is better to be careful. Let's walk by the side of the road." They began to walk, their footsteps light but quick, keeping close to the houses and the drain running parallel to the road. Once they crossed the rail tracks they came upon large wood-sheds, with long pieces of timber piled around them, some of them half-sawn. The damp smell of shavings was in the air. Bilkis remembered how she would come to the woodsheds as a child and gape in wonder at the logs being sawn. The wind would blow fine particles of sawdust straight into her eyes which would then smart and water.

She was not sure of their direction and asked, "Isn't the road to the movie hall up ahead?"

"Yes, you remember?"

"Yes, of course I do."

Siraj placed a finger on his lips to indicate that they should remain silent and went on, stopping from time to time to look around, scuttling across open areas and trying to blend into the surrounding bushes. Bilkis followed him, her question about where they were going still unanswered. Soon they entered an area that looked familiar and she broke the silence to ask, "Isn't this Mukhtar Para?"

"Yes, we're almost there."

Siraj stopped suddenly in front of a house and then quickly dragged her by the hand into a nearby shed. For the first time Bilkis heard the sound of a human being in Jaleswari, the sound of someone walking with a heavy measured tread down the gravel-strewn path in the distance. The two of them came out of the back of the shed and passed beneath a jackfruit tree to enter the large yard of a house. The darkness was far less congealed here and dried leaves were strewn everywhere. A fence on the left ran past a row of jackfruit trees. A tin shed lay to the right and a kitchen roof with a pile of hay and an empty cowshed next to it were visible at the end of the yard. The house, too, appeared as uninhabited as the cowshed.

"Isn't there anyone living here?"

"There is." Siraj whispered. Bilkis was taken by surprise because the house looked like it had not been lived in for some time.

Siraj indicated that Bilkis should wait and walked like a cat across the yard to the tin shed. It was then that Bilkis noted the figure of a man seated on a stool inside the shed, a man whom Siraj approached and exchanged words with. Then he came out and waved at her to come forward.

When she was near, Siraj told the man, "This is Kader Master's daughter."

The man did not appear to hear what he said and sat there like a statue, his eyes fixed on the yard in front. "This is Alif Mukhtar," Siraj whispered. "He has lost his vision."

A soft moan escaped Bilkis. Alif Mukhtar had been a renowned man around Jaleswari, the local Muslim League leader during British rule. Bilkis remembered the victory procession that had come out in Jaleswari, with a garlanded Alif Mukhtar at its head, after he won the election. In the year Pakistan was declared an independent state, Bilkis had won the first prize in recitation at the local girls' school on the occasion of an Eid reunion, and Alif Mukhtar had given her the prize. In 1954, when he lost the election to Qasem Miyan, Bilkis remembered how her mother had taunted her father, "Well, aren't you proud of your student? He's won the election, hasn't he? Why are you sad? Why don't you forget your friend of so many years and jump with joy at Qasem's victory? Let's see how proud of your student you really are." Bilkis remembered how embarrassed her father had looked.

This was the same Alif Mukhtar, staring vacantly with his sightless eyes into the leaf-strewn yard. Bilkis was at a loss for words.

"He sits like this all day." Siraj said.

The tin-roofed room contained two ancient almirahs and a large bed, the varnish still gleaming on it here and there in the dark. The room was also filled with a musty smell, the smell of clothes that had not dried properly.

"Isn't there anyone else in the house?"

"No."

"What about his family?"

"His daughter married someone from the navy, I don't know her whereabouts. Both his sons are in Pabna." Siraj paused and added, "In a mental hospital I am told. Just wait." Siraj went close to Alif Mukhtar and exchanged a few words with him before he came back.

"His wife?"

"I don't know why, but his wife has been at her parents' place for some time now. His blindness set in around the time she left."

"Doesn't she visit him?"

"Who knows? I haven't seen her."

"Then who looks after him? Who cooks and cleans for him?"

"His long-standing clerk used to do that. But he fled when the troubles started."

"And now?"

Siraj remained quiet and then said, with a dismissive laugh, "Who's there to look out for anyone these days?"

Bilkis was stunned at his callous response to the question of who was looking after a blind old man of nearly seventy. It seemed strange, coming from the same Siraj who had accompanied her on a journey fraught with danger all the way from Nabagram only because he worried for her safety.

Her legs ached and she felt her way in the dark to the bed and sat down upon it.

"Siraj, why did you laugh when I asked who was looking after old Mukhtar?"

Siraj appeared to smile briefly again and came closer. "I am not laughing, *Apa*. There is nothing funny about the state Alif Mukhtar is in. Do you want to know who looks after him these days? A bunch of Bihari hooligans."

"Bihari?" Bilkis started at the word. Where had Siraj brought her?

"Yes, some Bihari youth. The night before the military put in an appearance at Jaleswari, news spread of their coming. Those who could leave their homes fled across the river. Among the Bengalis only Alif Mukhtar was left behind. The Biharis came out in gangs once the army arrived, forcing their way into houses and ransacking them. One such gang found the Mukhtar Sahib and proceeded to make fun of his blindness. They strung a garland of shoes around his neck, fixed a '*Joy Bangla*' flag to his chest, attached a rope to his waist and paraded him around as an object of ridicule. The blind old man could barely walk and kept stumbling. His tormentors prodded him with sticks to bring him back to his feet, kicking and shoving him around before they were done with him and brought him back here. The next day they took him out again to repeat the show. They keep doing the same thing to him every now and then, keeping him alive with scraps of food only because of the fun they get out of him."

Bilkis listened to him in stunned silence.

"I heard that they had done the same thing to him today. Since then he has been sitting here without moving." Siraj paused. "They've looted whatever there was in the house and don't come inside any more. That's why I thought it fit to bring you here. They won't come back tonight. As you know, the best place to hide is right under the enemy's nose."

Bilkis was amazed at Siraj's wisdom. He seemed experienced beyond his years. She wondered briefly whether her brother was also a grown-up now.

Quietly she drew close to Alif Mukhtar. At her approach the blind man asked, "Who's there?" without moving his eyes from the yard.

"It's me."

The blind man remained quiet for a while. Siraj came and stood next to Bilkis. After what seemed like an eternity, Mukhtar cleared his throat, a sound that startled both of them. Then, with his eyes still upon the yard, he said in a surprisingly strong voice, "Your father used to be a good friend of mine."

He lapsed into silence after that and said no more, though Bilkis waited expectantly.

"Don't you want to come in and lie down?"

No reply.

"Do you want me to help you to bed?"

"Let him be here." Siraj sounded impatient. "Why don't you go in and I'll sit with him here."

Bilkis ignored him and addressed Mukhtar again.

Suddenly the old man burst into a lament. "Where do I go? To my grave?" He cried, "They killed so many boys today!"

"What? What did you say?" Bilkis cried out in fear.

"I am blind but I can still see their faces." Alif Mukhtar whimpered.

Siraj did something inexplicable. He grasped Bilkis's hand and dragged her back into the room. "Please stay inside!" he growled.

"No!" Bilkis stopped herself from falling, pushed him away and ran back to where the blind man sat. "Whom did they kill?" she demanded.

An image of Khoka filled her heart with agony. For the first time Alif Mukhtar turned his face from the yard, searched for her hand and clasped it firmly. With his weak, trembling touch he felt her hands and face. Then he said, "They were all lined up and shot in the market today. Wasn't your brother named Khoka?"

5

"Please come inside." Siraj's voice was grim and resonated in the silence. Bilkis stared uncomprehendingly, first at him and then at Alif Mukhtar. Then she went inside the room as directed. When Siraj told her to sit she was surprised to find herself sitting down docilely on a corner of the bed. Siraj stood before her for a while and then sat down next to her. Staring at a bright patch of light that fell upon the carvings on the almirah he said, "Your brother Khoka is dead. I didn't tell you. I had decided not to tell you." He buried his face in his hands and his body quivered with silent sobs. But Bilkis remained unmoved, as if a piece of information she already knew had simply been presented to her afresh.

When she placed her hand on Siraj's back, the boy's sobbing grew stronger. It seemed as if the weight of all the deaths he had witnessed or heard of in the past few months had come to haunt him.

"Khoka is no more?" Bilkis asked him calmly. She waited for Siraj to pull himself together and then asked, "What happened?"

"They lined up a number of boys in the market and shot them all together."

"Was Khoka among them?"

"Yes."

"When did you learn of this?"

"When I left you and went out. Mukhtar Sahib told me."

"Did he mention Khoka specifically?"

"Not by name. There were many, he said—Muhafiz, Nantoo, Irfan, Chuni Merchant's brother-in-law. And then he said, Kader Master's son too. Also several shopkeepers, a few children and some people who had simply come to shop."

"In the morning?"

"I am not sure of the time."

Bilkis remained immersed in her bewilderment for some time and then pressed on, "But Mukhtar cannot see. Somebody must have told him about the incident. Who was it?"

Without waiting for Siraj to reply, she got up to ask Mukhtar the same question.

"Where are you going? The Biharis who dragged him to the market with a rope around his waist were the ones who told him the names."

Just then the blind Mukhtar came inside, feeling his way in the dark. Bilkis got up to hold his hand and guide him to the bed. Mukhtar emitted a sigh of despair and sat down. Bilkis did not have the heart to pester him with questions.

But after some time Mukhtar began to speak. "I haven't heard of such bestiality. They have ordered that the corpses must lie where they were shot. Nobody can touch them. Those tender, young bodies will be torn apart by vultures and dogs without being allowed last rites."

"Who gave the order?"

"The military. Who else is there to give orders? But won't they have to die too one day? Hordes of Yazid! They snatched those young lives from their mothers' bosoms and now they would even deny them their final peace in the arms of Mother Earth! But they are fools, fools! They don't know that Mother Earth will surely pull her children to her bosom and angels of the Lord will perform their last rites. Their orders won't stand before the Lord's angels." Alif Mukhtar continued to mourn hoarsely—an inhuman wail that sounded more like the sighing of the wind or the lament of the night herself.

"Siraj, get up."

"*Apa*?"

"Come outside."

Siraj followed Bilkis outside and gave her an inquiring look. "Didn't you tell me that the military did not come out at night?" she asked.

"Why do you ask?"

"I'll go to the market. I have to see Khoka or his body with my own eyes to believe. I have to bury him with my own hands."

Siraj looked agitated.

"Will you come with me, Siraj?"

6

Siraj was taken aback by the unwavering, determined note in Bilkis's voice.

"Will you or won't you?"

"That is simply not possible, *Apa*!"

"If you won't come along, I will go on my own."

"It's not what you think," Siraj interposed hurriedly, "it's virtually impossible to get there without risking discovery in the open. The Biharis are roaming everywhere and they'll spot you."

"But how can I sit quietly while my own sibling lies dead without a proper burial?"

"You are acting crazy!"

"I have to go, Siraj."

"They have orders to shoot at sight."

"Let them shoot. One more corpse won't make a difference."

Siraj realized that this Bilkis was different from the woman he had thought he had come to know—she was now a stranger who stood undeterred against the might of the storm. He mulled things over. When he had gone out in the evening, leaving Bilkis in the deserted house, he had learned not just from Alif Mukhtar but also from Maqbool at the sweetshop that an order had been issued for the dead bodies to lie where they had fallen. Anybody who risked going near, let alone touch them, was to be shot. Whether this was a ploy to spread terror among the populace or a stratagem to seize whoever came near the bodies was not clear.

"Let me go on my own if you are afraid to come, Siraj. If I came all the way from Dacca only to hear of my brother's death, then I might as well see his dead body with my own eyes and give him a decent burial."

"Fine. If you aren't afraid, why should I care for myself?" The reply sounded more hurt and reproachful than filled with bravado.

Bilkis held Siraj by the hand and made him sit down. "Let me go and see what Mukhtar Sahib is up to," she said and went inside.

She found Mukhtar lying on the bed like a felled tree. She leaned close to his face to see if he was merely asleep or had given up the ghost altogether. She placed a hand gently on his chest and felt him breathing slowly, his heart beating very faintly. She stared at his face, unblinking, for some more time, remembering her own father and feeling strangely calm.

She came out and sat down next to Siraj. “When do you think is it a good time to leave?” she asked.

“A little later. Around midnight.”

“Don’t the Biharis come out on their rounds?”

“Not late at night. They may be Biharis and stooges of the army, but even they are afraid.”

“Afraid of what?”

“Of those who came in the dead of night and blew up the railway bridge. Of those who move around in the dark like shadows and disappear into the night after their raids without leaving a trace.”

Bilkis had witnessed this for herself in Dacca and also heard of the exploits of the patriots on the Free Bengal radio broadcasts.

“That’s why the army shot so many people in the market. To send out a message. But their deaths won’t remain unavenged, just wait and see.” Siraj sounded much less afraid now. Almost as if he, too, were ready to jump into the fray.

“Can I ask you something, Siraj? Why have you risked your own life on my behalf? I really don’t want anything bad to happen to you on my account. You’ve done enough as it is.”

Bilkis patted his hand gently, trying to gauge whether it was his impressionable youth that was impelling Siraj towards a misguided and romantic notion of chivalry. If so, she was prepared not to indulge him any further.

"Tell me," she persisted, "why did you accompany me all the way from Nabagram, risking your skin? What if you, too, had got caught like Khoka? What if they had killed you too?"

Siraj remained silent and let his head sink on to his chest. After some time he raised his head and said, "Yes, I too could have got caught."

"Then why did you come?"

"Because this is my work. I am working."

"What do you mean?"

Siraj grinned sheepishly and then grew serious. "I've told you about how I wanted to escape to India after I lost my parents and sister. But I couldn't pluck up the courage. For some weeks I remained on the run. One night, I heard some rumor that made me get up and leave in the middle of the night. *Didi*, I had to run across an area infested with poisonous snakes, an area I wouldn't have normally ventured into even by daylight. But I had no choice."

For the first time Bilkis noticed how Siraj used both the Bengali *didi* and the Urdu *apa*, terms which both literally meant 'elder sister,' when addressing her with the respect due an older woman. Jaleswari used to be a Hindu-dominated area at one time and even Muslim families were comfortable using the term *didi* in similar circumstances. The Urdu *apa* became popular after the land became Pakistan. Bilkis would not have noticed anything if Siraj had used one or the other term, but his awkward switching back and forth between the two made him appear younger than his years, a callow, overgrown teenager who was still not comfortable talking for a long time with an unknown lady.

"I expected to die of snakebite every moment," Siraj continued. "You know of the infamous cobras of Rangpur, don't you? But strangely enough I survived. The next day I told myself that I won't run away to India. I decided to stay on in my homeland, where I have lost my family. See things through to the end."

"You are very brave."

"I am not brave, *Apa*. My friends who went off to India at the beginning underwent training there and came back to fight the military—they are the brave ones." Siraj paused and appeared to be thinking of his friends. Then he emitted a long sigh.

"What is it?" Bilkis asked.

"Nothing."

"But you are brave. Otherwise, you wouldn't have come with me to Jaleswari even after hearing of the bridge being destroyed."

"I came because Mansur-*da* told me to."

"Who is he?"

"I wanted to tell you earlier, but lost my train of thought. I work with Mansur-*da* to help those who come across the border. After the bridge was blown up a trainload of soldiers came in today. I had the duty of keeping an eye on arrivals and departures at Nabagram station. That's how I spotted you on the afternoon train."

"Yes, I noticed how you went behind the bushes after seeing me on the platform."

"You were different from the other passengers. It was easy to make out that you came from Dacca."

"Really?"

"Yes. I went and informed Mansur-*da*, who came and took a look at you through the station house window. He took one look and told me, 'This is my teacher Kader Master's daughter.'"

"So your Mansur-*da* was my father's student?"

"Yes, he is the grandson of Paran the hawker—the one whom the British gave a medal. I have seen that medal in their house. Mansur-*da* told me, 'Maybe she wants to go to Jaleswari. Try to dissuade her. But if she insists, then escort her there.'"

"How come he did not come forward himself?"

"He has other things to do. Also, it would be risky for him to go to Jaleswari after the raid on the bridge. That's why he sent me and that's why I urged you not to come here. But you didn't listen."

"Fine, your Mansur-*da* could have told you to take me to Jaleswari. But he didn't tell you to help me bury Khoka's body, did he?"

Siraj appeared immersed in thought.

"Would you come with me even if he forbade you to?"

Siraj appeared to be in a quandary. Finally he said, "I have a feeling that in my position he too would have come along with you."

"Why do you say so?"

"Something that you said is stuck in my mind."

"What?"

"About how you couldn't rest so long as your brother's corpse lay unclaimed in the market." A deep note of remorse now sounded in Siraj's voice as he said, "*Apa*, I think I am a low-grade coward."

"Why do you say that?"

"Otherwise why would I leave my folks and run, knowing very well that their lives wouldn't be spared? Wasn't I a coward to leave them all and flee? Clearly I have neither your courage nor your attachment towards your family."

Bilkis noticed tears in his eyes and hastened to intervene. "Don't talk that way," she told him, "I, too, used to fear for my life once upon a time. If my husband Altaf were alive today, I too would have thought first and foremost of his safety and mine. But with Altaf gone, I have lost my fear and my grief too. I have shed no tears since I heard that Khoka has been killed and that his corpse is lying in the market with nobody allowed to touch it. But why not? Wouldn't my life have been smashed to smithereens even six months back if I had heard the same? Yet now I am still on my feet, thinking calmly of how to bury his body. Nobody is intrinsically a coward, Siraj. Nobody buckles under grief and fear all the time. Remember that." She remained quiet for a while and asked, "When do we leave?"

Siraj, who appeared lost in a reverie, stood up with a start. "Let me first go and take a look around," he said.

"How far will you go?"

"Not very far. Up to the crossroads ahead. Didn't you hear the footsteps some time ago? That was the vigilantes of the Peace Committee making their rounds. It will be hard to proceed so long as they are still around. But they don't usually hang around very long. Still, I'd better go and ensure that they are gone."

Siraj walked silently across the yard and was soon lost in the darkness beyond the fence. Suddenly Bilkis felt her heart skip a beat. The vision of Khoka lying in a pool of his own congealed blood rose before her eyes as clearly as if she could see him herself.

She felt warm tears rolling down her cheek.

7

The town of Jaleswari lay silent and empty like a village abandoned after an outbreak of plague. Not even a dog was in sight. Bilkis and Siraj crept noiselessly in the dark to stand near the back of a shuttered *paan* shop standing at the crossroads and looked down the main road branching off. The moon was in the sky and in the pallid glow she cast the road looked strangely still and unreal.

A sound was heard in the distance.

"They are still around," whispered Siraj. They instinctively stiffened in alarm since the source of the sound could not be traced and there was no way to know if they had risked discovery or not. A sound could appear abnormally loud in the stillness of the night and it was easy enough to mistake the direction it came from. So they peered hurriedly to the left and right and even where the wall of a derelict Kali temple rose behind them.

"They seem to be patrolling quite seriously."

"If only we could see them."

They could then have seized the right moment to cross the road. But it would be foolhardy to risk discovery now. They might still cross over by the time the shooting started, but the sentinels would get an alert and give chase. It was more sensible to wait.

"Siraj?"

"Yes?"

"You can still go back." Bilkis whispered, her ears still on the sound. Siraj said nothing.

"Is Khoka really dead?"

"Maqbool-*da* said as much."

"What else did Mukhtar Sahib tell you? About Khoka?"

"I can't tell you."

"You can. I can bear it."

Siraj thought it over. The sound of a leaf snapping in the plantain grove next to the Kali temple was heard.

"What was that?"

"A leaf snapping in the grove. They took Mukhtar to where Khoka's corpse lay and told him that it belonged to Kader Master's son. Then they prodded him on the abdomen repeatedly."

"Why?"

Siraj hesitated.

"Why did they prod him?"

"They wanted the old man to urinate on the corpse." Bilkis felt something choking her.

"They prodded him till he lost sense. But they themselves must have done it."

Bilkis shivered. "Why, Siraj? Why were they so brutal with him? What had Khoka done?"'

Siraj placed a warning finger on his lips, advancing stealthily and poking his head out from behind the shop's wall. Then he motioned Bilkis to come forward.

"Follow me. I'll cross the road first. Come only after you see me waving from the other side."

Siraj crawled most of the way across the road and vanished among the houses. But soon his blurred figure was visible on the other side, summoning her silently.

As she crossed the road in the pale moonlight, Bilkis felt suspended momentarily between life and death. Only when she was back in the darkness did she feel warm and secure. Without a word Siraj led her by the hand and threaded his way between the houses till they reached a stagnant, muddy patch. A dog could be heard barking in the distance, the only sound after the footsteps of the patrolling men. They waited for the dog to bark louder and warn the patrol of their presence.

"That's why I headed straight for this place. Otherwise we would be in trouble." There was suppressed triumph in Siraj's voice for having successfully evaded discovery. The dog stopped barking.

"*Apa*, we'll have to proceed carefully, staying close to the edge of the swamp. There's hardly any place to walk and if you miss your footing you'll be in the mud."

On the far side of the swamp lay the abandoned, single-storeyed residence of the Sinhas, who had gone away to Calcutta long ago. Even the priest of the Kali temple who had taken up residence there was now gone. Broken doors and windows stood visible as ghostly structures in the moonlight.

"Please hold my hand."

They took the first few steps gingerly before they became more confident and picked up speed. The idea was to cross beyond the swamp into the locality of Kachheri Para and cover the remaining distance by foot.

Bilkis emitted a muffled exclamation as her foot sank into the mud. Siraj pulled at her hand and the soft plop of her foot coming out of the squelchy mud was heard. Bilkis could also be heard breathing hard.

"Wait let me fix my sari."

"Do it when we are on the other side. There may be reptiles here."

Once they reached the other side, Bilkis stopped, panting. "Do you want to rest?" Siraj asked.

"No, no."

She found herself in an unfamiliar part of the town she had been born in. She had no idea that there was such a large copse behind Kachheri Para, a veritable thicket of mango, lychee and *jamun* trees. At one time this used to be the orchard of the Bakshis.

"It's safe to go through the Bakshis' orchard, *Apa*. But you must be careful not to walk on dry leaves—they'll crackle. We are going to take this shortcut and come up right behind the post office. Then we take the street to the market."

Bilkis mused how the hesitant Siraj of a short while ago was now so confidently in charge. The woods looked strange in the moonlight.

"Why were they so brutal with Khoka? You didn't tell me," she asked again.

"He used to sing very well."

"Yes, he sang twice for the Rangpur radio station. His dream was to sing for the Dacca station and he had wanted to go there. Did you know Khoka?"

"I knew of him. I didn't know him personally."

"Why did they act like such beasts?"

"Maybe because of his singing. He was the one who taught *Amar Sonar Bangla* to everyone around here. He would head the processions that took place in March, leading the chorus. That was why he was spotted."

"Why didn't he run away?"

"Not everybody could. I couldn't."

"Maybe because of my mother. She was old."

"I wonder how Khoka *Bhai* got caught. He used to stay indoors most of the time."

"Was he caught in the house?"

"No. Maqbool-*da* said that when our boys went around the houses, urging people to leave, Khoka *Bhai* wasn't home."

"Where was he then?"

The two of them had nearly crossed the orchard and the yellow walls of the post office were visible through the leaves. A grove of bamboos stood next to the post office, the stalks standing tall and rigid like flagpoles barren of flags.

8

Now they came upon the sight they had dreaded so long—bodies strewn all around the open square of the marketplace, bodies clutching in death at fences, lying face downward in the lane, which sloped away from the square. Rows upon rows of corpses—of children who had tried to take cover behind an upturned cart, of fruit-sellers whose wicker baskets lay here and there among earthen vessels and scattered vegetables—all reigned over by a stillness that spoke of the total inability of an everyday scene to ever come back to life.

The two of them stared dumbstruck at a vision that appeared to lie beyond the understanding of reality, yet immediate and present. Then, almost in unison, impelled by the same emotions, they looked at each other. Siraj covered his face with his hands and sank to the ground, resting his head against a fence.

Bilkis kept staring at the square, lit by the fickle, cloud-capped moonlight. The anger that had simmered within her since she had heard of the desecration of Khoka's body now flashed like an angry sword, dimming everything with its glow except the bodies lying in front of her. She began to advance towards them. Something shadowy moved ahead of her, but she remained oblivious to anything but the body which lay across her path in the near distance. Soon she came out of the shade of a jute godown, followed by her own shadow. Siraj stood up slowly as he watched her with amazement, a woman making her ghostly progress down a row of what appeared to be sleeping bodies, a woman not of the past or the present or even the future, but an image lit up momentarily by arrested time before it faded into the night. He looked up and saw a band of grey clouds racing in to obscure the moon one by one. As they engulfed the moonlight, he could no longer see Bilkis. The bodies were barely visible, appearing as isolated clumps of darkness before his eyes.

He ran into the square looking for Bilkis but could not locate her, as if she had been pulled into the silence or claimed as one of their own by the dead. Then he stumbled and found that he had run into her, kneeling beside a corpse and trying to examine its face. It was the corpse of a middle-aged peasant, the eyes still open, dried blood at the corner of the mouth and teeth visible almost as if bared in a smile.

Siraj helped Bilkis to her feet, saying softly, "*Apa.*"

"So many bodies, Siraj." Bilkis spoke in a steady voice. Siraj cast a terrified look around him and quickly pulled her behind a shed. "Have you taken leave of your senses?" He spoke in an admonishing tone. "You have no idea who might be lurking around here."

"No, there's no one."

"How can you be sure?"

"A jackal just scampered off. No jackal would have come near if there had been people around."

Siraj pricked his ears for unusual sounds, but heard nothing except the faint gargle of the water in the nearby canal, a sound that in the silence seemed to course more in his soul than through his ears.

"But still, you have to be careful. They could be lying in hiding anywhere, with orders to shoot whoever approaches the bodies."

"I know."

"Don't imagine that they have simply left the bodies to rot and gone away."

"Siraj, go back."

"And you?"

"I will locate Khoka. Give him a burial."

The moon broke free of the clouds and lit up the square with the azure whiteness of a shroud.

"I am not afraid to die, Siraj. I can ignore their orders." Bilkis said.

Siraj stared into her face for some time and said, "*Apa*, do you think that I fear for my life? Haven't they killed my father? Didn't they take away my sister?"

Bilkis placed a restraining hand on his shoulder and said, "Stop. Don't cry."

"I am not crying for myself. I don't want to lose another sister, that's all."

Bilkis understood and quickly drew him tenderly to her bosom. "Don't cry. Please. Don't you think I want you next to me, helping me bury Khoka together as his brother and sister would?"

Finally their world, which had been severely shaken by the scene they had encountered at the last bend of the market road, beyond the row of jute warehouses and the tin sheds of the traders, appeared to resume a semblance of stability. An objective, distant but clear, seemed to take shape before their eyes.

The two of them went back to the square silently. "You are right," Bilkis whispered, "if we get caught then we can no longer bury Khoka."

"*Apa*, let's not linger here and attract attention. It's better that we crawl."

"I don't want to get caught, Siraj. I don't. I want to evade capture so that I can give Khoka a decent burial and prove that he is not a pariah whose body can lie unclaimed and dishonored." Bilkis spoke slowly, pausing as she crawled from one body to another, lifting the head to identify the corpse and lowering it to the ground again. Not every corpse had to be identified this way. Sometimes it was easy enough to make out a shopkeeper, a porter or an ordinary villager by the clothes they wore.

Both of them started when they saw a body lying in the distance, clad in trousers and a half-sleeved shirt, in the posture of someone who had doubled over from a pain in the stomach. The body appeared to be that of a youth.

"Khoka?"

Siraj took a look at the face and emitted a muffled exclamation.

"Who is it?"

"Irfan."

Bilkis gently lowered the head.

"He was a good footballer, so he couldn't complete his studies. He had set up a library in the market."

Close by lay the body of another youth, the face turned away, the legs curled up under the chest, much as they would if he were snug in bed on a winter night under a blanket. Only one hand stretched upward, taut and straight.

"Nantoo."

"Which family is he from?"

"He's the elder son of Bhola the doctor."

Bilkis remembered Bhola the doctor, who had prescribed medicines for her when she was young. Sometimes, on her demand, he would even part with some of his white, sweet pellets on his own. He had been the most well-known homeopath in Jaleswari.

"I haven't seen Nantoo in a while." She said. She stared back at the face and even placed a hand on the cheek, amazed at how the little Nantoo she had known had grown into a big boy who shaved. The face slowly began to resemble the memory she had of the child.

"How he had grown."

Siraj averted his face. After some time he whispered hoarsely, "We don't have much time, *Apa*."

"Wait, let me arrange Nantoo's body properly."

They crawled around some more in the dark but failed to come across Khoka's body.

"Siraj, do you think they took his body away?"

"I don't think so."

"Was he really here?"

"Both Maqbool-*da* and Alif Mukhtar said so. I told you about what they wanted Mukhtar to do."

Bilkis's anger surged back and she straightened up. "Listen, Siraj . . . " she began. Something in her voice scared Siraj. As he got up, Bilkis held his hand in a firm grip and said, "We are going to bury all the bodies. Yes, all of them."

"Shouldn't we search for Khoka *Bhai*?"

"We don't have to. He must be here. As we bury them one by one, we'll find Khoka."

The two of them stared at each other in silence. Then Bilkis said, "We have to find a place first." She did not have to elaborate what she was talking of.

Siraj thought for a while and said, "We can't go very far. The soil by the canal is soft. I hope burying the bodies there won't be against your customs."

Bilkis stared at him, surprised and said, "Our customs?"

"What I meant," Siraj replied hurriedly, "is that I don't know whether it is right to bury a body outside a graveyard and wondered if it would be dishonoring the dead to bury them by the canal. Anyway, let me go and take a look."

Bilkis stared at him as he went, unable to shrug off the surprise she had felt. Then she turned around, and one look at the square brought back the brutal reality that dominated all other thought. As she looked at the bodies her mind tried to picture the scene of murder and mayhem that would have taken place in the afternoon. Alif Mukhtar had spoken of the boys being lined up and shot. It was easy to make out from the positions of Nantoo's and Irfan's bodies that they had been in the same line. Had Khoka not been in the same line then? Had a second line been formed? Maybe a third?

Then she saw a few other scattered corpses with baskets of vegetables lying near them—people who appeared to have been shot while trying to escape—and wondered who had been shot first, the ones put into a line or the ones who had made a dash for it.

"*Apa*, there's a big hole dug by the canal. Do you want to see it?"

A lane wound its way through rows of shops on either side towards the canal. None of the shops had its shutters down and cupboards and shelves lay starkly open and vandalized. The shops had all been looted, just the same way as on previous such occasions. Bilkis walked down the lane without showing any fear of discovery. She appeared to have forgotten the risk or was convinced that there was no one to see them.

The hole Siraj thought had been dug was not a real hole at all but a declivity created by the periodic removal of earth to prop up the dykes that lined the canal to protect against flooding.

Bilkis lowered herself into it and examined the soft, fine earth mixed with sand. Siraj looked at her with curiosity.

"We have to dig more on the other side," Bilkis said after she had walked around the hollowed area. "It will accommodate a maximum of eight or nine of them. We'll have to dig a bigger grave."

"Why don't we fill this one up first?"

"All right."

Siraj looked around for something sharp to dig with, but there was nothing. "We might find something in the market," Bilkis said and the two of them retraced their steps. They went into a few shops to search for picks or shovels, inured by now to the sight of the dead bodies around them, which merely appeared to be waiting peacefully for their rites of passage.

They came across a piece of tin, with a faint smell of fish scales lingering on it. One of the fishmongers would have used it to cover his catch.

"This will do."

"We need one more."

Following the smell of fish, they went further ahead. Finding a few more similar pieces of tin, they went back quickly to the canal. The earth was not as soft and unyielding as it had appeared at first. The soil underneath the covering of sand had a hard and clumpy layer. Bilkis and Siraj were soon covered with clods of earth, but they dug away undeterred as the fickle moonlight sometimes aided them and at other times vanished behind clouds.

After digging for half an hour, Bilkis stood up and said, "That's it." She realized that her back was aching and sat down, resting against the slope of the hole. Siraj too was drenched in sweat and sat down next to her, wiping his forehead.

"Have you noticed that there's not a single sentry anywhere around?" Bilkis observed.

"So I see." Siraj cast a cautious look around nevertheless and even peered at the far side of the canal where a field of crops ended in a black band of trees.

"Considering the orders, it would have seemed that this place would be guarded round the clock. Strange."

"What's so strange, Siraj? Even they fear the dark."

But Siraj did not lower his guard and continued to be watchful. Bilkis got up to her feet and said, "They are afraid to follow their own decrees."

"I still think we should hurry." Siraj too rose to his feet. They climbed up the slope and looked down upon the grave below them, whose gaping emptiness seemed to mimic and even exceed in depth the emptiness of the reality they faced.

A corpse straddled the lane where it merged into the square—the corpse of a rustic woman whose short sari had risen above her knees, whose breasts were exposed and whose jaw was set at an unnatural angle. Half her face was covered with straggly hair. Without any discussion they decided to begin with her and got to work. Gently, as if she did not want the woman to wake up, Bilkis extricated her arms from under her body.

"Hold her feet, Siraj."

But they did not find it easy to lift her. The human body seemed to get heavier once it died, as if the soul, when present, granted lightness to it, with the possibility of wafting upwards like a bird. In the absence of life and dreams, the human body was but a deadweight. They had no option but to gently drag the body down the lane and the slope and deposit it in a corner of the grave. Then they returned to the square to bring the next body, picking up whoever came first. This way they managed to lower six bodies into the grave. While Bilkis had estimated the grave to be large enough for eight or nine bodies, it was full with six. Both of them were beset by exhaustion and the realization that they needed a grave far bigger than this one. Bilkis said with a sigh, "Maybe a couple of children here . . . " pointing to the vacant space near the feet of the bodies.

"You wanted the heads to point to the north. The children can't be placed that way," Siraj interjected.

"Doesn't matter. Hurry."

Each of them cradled the body of a child and came back to the bank of the canal. Suddenly a pair of eyes, gleaming in the dark, was visible on the far side. For a moment their blood ran cold but then they realized that the eyes probably belonged to a jackal, which did not fear the presence of two live people among so many who were dead. Or maybe the animal had sensed that the two of them were nearly dead too with fatigue anyway.

They came out of the grave after placing the children in it. Before filling up the hole with earth Bilkis asked Siraj if he knew which *surah* or prayer was uttered before a grave was covered. Siraj remained quiet, simply staring with a mesmerized look at the row of bodies before him.

"Do you believe in Allah?" She asked him.

Siraj's lips quivered with emotion. "No," he replied.

Bilkis glanced at him and then found her own mouth widening in a smile that came from within, unbeknownst, to her.

"Then let's simply say, 'return, then, to the earth whence thou once came . . . .'" The two of them bent forward, scooped up earth in their hands and allowed it to drop gently between their fingers into the grave below. Once their hands became empty, they continued to stand still for a long time.

"Siraj?"

"*Didi*?"

"Call me either *apa* or *didi*. Get going, don't we have to fill this up?"

They had barely managed to cover half the grave with the earth they could scoop up with their hands. They used the shards of tin to prise out more soil from the slope of the canal bank to fill it up.

Just then they heard staccato bursts of gunfire in the distance.

9

Bilkis and Siraj dropped to the ground at once, flattening themselves against the slope of the canal bank. The firing seemed to come first from the far side and then from the direction of the market. It stopped soon, but the sound continued to resonate in the ensuing silence for some time.

"Where is it coming from?"

"Can't make out."

The firing did not resume and everything appeared to get back to normal. Nor could they hear any voices or footsteps from the direction of the market. Slowly they released their grip on the slope and allowed their bodies to slide down into the grave. There did not appear to be enough time to fill it up and level the earth. They had no idea where an attack might come from next.

"I don't think it's wise to stay here, Siraj."

"We need to know where the gunshots came from."

"Could be far away."

"They didn't sound all that far."

"So many bodies still left to bury."

"I wish we could have located Khoka *Bhai*."

"We'll bury him too, Siraj. We won't go back till that is done."

"But the night will end soon," Siraj whispered fearfully.

"Then we'll have to start again tomorrow."

"But it won't be safe to go away from here. We should hide somewhere in the marketplace."

"Here? Won't that be dangerous?"

"We are face to face with much bigger danger right now. The marketplace seems to be quiet."

Bilkis pricked up her ears and noted that the market appeared to be silent.

"Let's fill up this grave first," she suggested, "and tell ourselves that we did a job well."

"*Apa*, something just struck me."

"What?"

"We risked everything to come here and bury the dead. But does that really matter to the dead?"

"Who says it doesn't?"

"I don't see what difference it can make."

"That's because you are viewing those dead bodies as forms distinct from your own. But the moment you think of them as part of you, and yourself as part of them, you'll realize that by performing their last rites, we are honoring life itself."

They used the makeshift tin implements to level the earth over the grave. Then they followed the lane back to the market. When they came to the square they halted and took a cautious look around. They saw no one and everything seemed as they had left it. But still they moved carefully, taking care to blend into the shadows under the roofs of shops as well as they could.

"Where do we hide?"

"I have thought of a place, Siraj. Come with me."

Once they crossed the square and came to the row of jute warehouses, Bilkis turned and gazed at the bodies still lying in the square.

"Siraj, I wish we could have buried all of them today and shown those killers just how far their writ runs. They would have known that we are not animals. We don't leave our dead lying around to be eaten by vultures." Bilkis paused and then added, "But unfortunately we only have two hands and there are many bodies."

"Do you just want to stand here?"

"No, of course not."

"The sky is getting light."

"Siraj, I was thinking of hiding in one of these warehouses."

"All day?"

"As many days as necessary. I cannot leave till I've buried Khoka and the rest."

The doors to the warehouses were sealed with heavy padlocks. Siraj pulled on a few, in case one of them was unlocked by any chance. Finally they spotted a small warehouse next to the office of the traders, whose doors seemed to have been fastened only with rope. They approached the warehouse carefully and gently, very gently, Siraj pushed the doors open. He entered first, followed by Bilkis.

The moment they entered it was like being singed by hot flames. Their senses were assailed by the strong smell of jute till they felt dizzy. The darkness ahead of them was impregnable.

"We can't stay here long, *Apa*," Siraj hissed.

"We have to."

"This place is too hot and stuffy because of the jute. You'll die of suffocation if you stay here all day."

"Close the door behind you."

Siraj went back and shut the door. At once the interior was plunged in darkness. Siraj groped his way forward and whispered, "*Apa*." There was no response and he continued to grope ahead, making his way through piles of jute, till he found his progress blocked. Once again he called out, "*Apa*!" Suddenly he felt he was sinking into a nightmare from which he would never escape. Bilkis seemed to have left him to die here. He would have cried out in terror had he not heard her voice at that moment.

"Siraj, where are you?"

Siraj backed away till he found himself in a relatively open space. He felt Bilkis's hand brush against his and grabbed it quickly. "It's so dark, *Apa*!" he murmured.

"Are you afraid?"

"I couldn't hear you, that's why."

"I groped around on the other side. The whole room is packed with bales of jute. We need to drag a couple of bales to the door and block the entrance against any possible intruder. Come."

Bilkis led him by the hand to a pile of bales on the left. It took a superhuman effort to shift a bale from the stack to the door. But the precarious situation they were in lent them strength and they managed to block the door eventually.

"Maybe we need to use one more."

They dragged a second bale to the door. A slight wind blew in from somewhere near the doorway, which made the heat more bearable. But they could not risk being anywhere near the door. Bilkis led Siraj by the hand back into the cavernous darkness of the warehouse along a narrow path that led deep within between piles of jute stacked on either side. After some time she stopped and sat down on the floor. "Sit down."

Siraj moved a little further away to avoid stumbling over her and sat down.

"Where are you?"

"Here."

"I would often come to a jute warehouse to play hide and seek when I was a child. The fun was that no matter how much you walked around or spoke, so long as you weren't very loud nobody inside, let alone outside, could hear you. I remembered this childhood game as soon as I thought of where to hide. I almost went back to that game as I was groping around. You said some time ago that you didn't believe in Allah, but if there hadn't been a higher being above, do you think things would have worked out for us the way they have so far?" Bilkis waited for a reply and said, "Why don't you say something?"

"If there was someone above, do you think my parents would have been killed, my sister raped or your brother lying dead in the market? Have you heard the bulletins on the Free Bengal radio about the genocide that has taken place? Hundreds of thousands have been killed. How many did you bury today with your own hands? And how many more are still left, with orders given for their bodies not to be touched? You say there's a higher being up there? Who? There's no one. Even if there is, that someone is on their side, not ours."

Siraj fell silent. Bilkis wondered whether she herself believed in Allah anymore. Did it really matter whether she too had lost her faith in Him, so long as she remained calm and did her duty? Why had she brought up Allah? Maybe from force of habit, or from something ingrained in her blood. But had she not bid adieu to Allah long back? Had she remembered Him even once from the moment she stepped into Jaleswari and faced all the trials and tribulations?

"Siraj?" There was no reply. "Are you angry with me?"

Bilkis searched for his face in the dark and touched his chin with her fingers. Stroking it lightly, she said, "I feel bad for you. But you aren't alone. I have no idea where my mother is, or my sister and her children. I've lost my brother and heard how they spat and urinated on his tender face. I don't know myself whether I am a widow. One part of my mind tells me that Altaf is alive, but another part wails loudly that he is gone. Sadly, this is the part that had once believed in Allah and justice and taken comfort from the notion that humanity still lives among men."

Siraj abruptly clutched her hand. Bilkis found the sudden, physical action unexpected. But the next minute Siraj released his grasp and drew away. "*Didi*, I have told you a lie," he spoke quietly, an admission that sounded even more unexpected.

"I am not Siraj. Mansur-*da*'s given me this name. My real name is Pradip."

"Pradip?"

"Pradip Kumar Biswas."

"And you are still here?"

"Yes. I didn't run away to India. Because I want to become Pradip here again someday. Can you now understand my pain? The pain of losing my family, my name and my identity, all of them in one night? We are told that our religion lends us protection. Did my religion protect me?"

Bilkis could not hear his words. Her mind was diverted to the bits of information about the boy it had been automatically processing since the evening—his words, behavior, reactions and different ways of addressing her all began to revolve inside her head.

"Pradip," she said, finally.

"*Didi*?"

"Who says that you are a coward? I am so proud of you."

10

The night gave way to daylight outside, but the inside of their shelter remained dark. Only later, when the sun grew strong overhead, did a faint light penetrate inside, an unreal dusk in which two human beings lay asleep at two ends of a narrow path weaving in between bales of jute, wrapped in sleep, the younger sibling of death and as complete and inevitable, as it smoothened the toils, shocks and grief of the night before. They remained oblivious to the turmoil that raged outside—the Biharis discovering that the corpses numbered fewer than before, their surprise and furore, the arrival of the soldiers, the discovery of the mass grave by the canal already dug up by jackals, warning shots fired in the air by the soldiers. None of these could disrupt the balm of sleep that enveloped them. When the Biharis proposed burning down a Bengali neighborhood to teach the rebels a lesson, the commanding major of the local army camp turned them down with a curt "No." Nor did the major tell them that during the night an army jeep with three passengers had been blown up after driving into a minefield on the only road linking Jaleswari with Rangpur, instantly killing all three. The Biharis still looked for Bengalis hiding in Jaleswari and, finding no one, walked into Alif Mukhtar's house, tied a noose around his neck and strangled him to death. But unknown to all of them, two of the Bengalis they were searching for continued to sleep in their sanctuary in the market. In the relative security of daylight, gun-toting Biharis patrolled the market square outside the warehouse where they lay hidden, while their friends and cousins sat a safe distance away from the fallen bodies, joking and smoking, some of them wearing the slim necklaces of *zari* that had come into fashion among them ever since the army had taken over Jaleswari.

11

Without food or water, they waited for night to come. Though Bilkis had spoken of how it was virtually impossible for anyone outside to hear anything going on inside the stuffy confines of the warehouse, they made sure not to make any noise once they woke up and found themselves in their cell padded with rough-textured jute fiber and heard the sound of voices and footsteps outside. Still grimy with sweat and mud from the previous night's excursion, the two figures sat still with bated breath all day. Gradually the hubbub outside subsided, evening came, and an unbroken silence dropped down to reign once again. The two of them, who had sat at a distance from each other so long, drew closer as they sensed the silence outside, their breath quickened and, touching hands, they waited eagerly.

Bilkis was the first to speak though her voice sounded unnatural and hoarse after such a prolonged silence. "We have to finish our job tonight," she whispered in Siraj's ear. He was worried stiff wondering whether the grave had been discovered and what reaction it might have evoked. In the impregnable darkness of the warehouse he could not make out Bilkis's face when she spoke. His inability to see her brought back the fear of death and the ponderous tolling of a knell stretching far and wide.

Time passed. Whether fifteen minutes, five hours, or indeed, a lifetime, nobody could fathom.

Bilkis got up and made a survey. Once she came back she whispered, "There's a hole in the wall over there. There's nobody around outside. I checked carefully."

The two of them wrestled with and moved the bales of jute that were blocking the doorway and crawled out. Once outside, they sat by the door, allowing the gentle breeze to clean their bodies and spirits of mud, grime and exhaustion till they felt whole and cleansed. Then they crawled ahead cautiously, turning the corner of the warehouse, crossing the narrow lane, and reaching the square. Craning her neck, Bilkis noted that the scene was no different from the previous night. The bodies lay as before, amid elongated shadows that looked like bodies themselves. The half-moon from the previous night could also be seen in the sky, emerging from behind the shaggy heads of trees behind the market. She signaled at Siraj to come forward and examine the scene. Gesturing silently with her chin, Bilkis asked him if they should move forward. Siraj gave a silent nod. They crawled on till they gradually regained their rhythm, confidence and sense of direction, and got to their feet near the entrance to a row of shops.

Now they could see further ahead, and many more corpses came into view. Tonight they could also sense the stench the bodies gave out, which was neither the smell of putrefaction, nor the benzoic aroma of preservative, but, rather, a melancholy smell of demise.

Their senses remained alert to the slightest sound or movement, but there was nothing save the momentary flight of a jackal, maybe from the night before, followed by a second one, in the distance. The world appeared to have been deserted by the living. Reassured, Bilkis whispered, "They wouldn't have come near if anybody was around." Siraj, too, found the sign comforting.

Leaving the entrance to the shops behind them, they proceeded further, driven by an urge they could not identify. Bilkis was looking for Khoka, thought Siraj. "We haven't checked the other side," Bilkis said, pointing ahead. They crossed the area redolent with the smell of fish scales and came to an area where two bodies lay supine with some distance between them. Although the thought crossed their minds that one of the bodies could be Khoka's, neither of them took the initiative to move forward, silently willing the other to be the first. Finally both turned their faces away. The square littered with bodies had begun to assume the aspect of familiarity, and they had begun to view the scene with the disinterest of spectators. Even the dead seemed to view the presence of the living with the same lack of interest.

They returned to the middle of the square, keeping close to the walls of the shops on the eastern side and stopped. Once again, they gazed at the scene before them, much as they would look out from the porch of their own house at the scenery outside.

"Siraj?"

"*Didi*?"

Bilkis was brought back to reality by this address. She corrected herself and called him Pradip. Simultaneously, the boy addressed her as '*Apa*' and they looked at each other, the innocence of their exchange temporarily holding their attention. The next moment, Bilkis said sadly. "I am going to call you Siraj," silently hoping for the day when she could call him Pradip again. "Khoka's body could be lying over there, where we were."

"I thought so too."

"Do you think they've worked out that we buried some of the bodies last night?"

Siraj remained silent.

"Will you take me back to Nabagram once this is over?"

"Nabagram?"

"To your Mansur-*da*?"

Siraj remained silent again.

"I want to be part of the movement, Siraj."

"Don't you want to cross the river and visit the far side?"

Bilkis could not understand the context and asked, "Why?"

"To look for your mother and sister?"

Bilkis was reminded of her other relatives. Strangely, she felt nothing for them, beyond wishing that they were safe and well.

"I want to do it for them too. And for all those lying dead here. Let's get to work. We mustn't leave a single body behind tonight."

Siraj had expected that they would return to the two newly discovered bodies. Instead, Bilkis went up to the body which lay closest to them, curled up at an angle. Bilkis straightened the figure with her own hands and made it lie straight on its back.

"Let's bring all the bodies and place them side by side here."

They got busy moving the bodies one by one and arranging them next to each other. Time passed and the moon climbed higher in the cloudless sky, its pallid, bloodless light falling on some parts of the square.

Once the square was empty they looked with tired eyes upon the row of corpses lying before them, forgetting their natural, human tendency to count the number. Then they went to the end of the square, where they had seen the two bodies in the night.

Bilkis realized that she had not seen Khoka for a long time. Their last exchange had been the letter he had sent her in anger after being denied the money he had asked her for to buy a new harmonium. Now she stooped over his body and stared at him fixedly. His blue shirt was crumpled near the chest, and she smoothed it with her hand.

"Here's Khoka, Siraj."

Siraj dropped down next to her and, placing both hands on the ground, peered at his face.

"He used to sing so well."

Siraj kept quiet.

"He asked me for some money for a harmonium. He loved our mother so much that he refused to come and stay with me in Dacca."

With her hand on Khoka's chest, Bilkis silently began to fight with the gaping emptiness inside her, till she suddenly felt something hard pressing against her back. She uttered a soft exclamation and turned her head. Behind her stood the shadowy figures of four young men armed with guns.

12

Woken from his sleep, the major in command of the local garrison came up to them rubbing his eyes. He had gone to sleep in his uniform and now he stared at Bilkis and Siraj with a quizzical look as he fastened his belt. Their captors stood at a distance, staring with curiosity and not a little envy from time to time at the major's uniformed frame and the steady, sharp look in his eyes. Turning towards them, the major ordered them to depart with a tired gesture. Disappointed, the four men left the scene after some hesitation.

The familiar classroom of section IXB in the Jaleswari High School began to look unfamiliar to Siraj.

The major sat down on a chair and stretched his legs. Without any hurry he raised a finger and indicated that they should come forward. An armed sentry stood guard at the door with a short, stout gun. Bilkis took a few steps forward and stopped when motioned by the major. Siraj was also asked to step forward. He took a step and stopped. The finger moved again and he took a few more steps forward.

When the major considered the distance between them and him satisfactory, he gave Siraj a stern glare, which contrasted with the bemused smile playing on his lips. Softly he asked in English, "Who is she?"

Siraj remained silent.

The question was repeated, this time in Urdu, addressed at Bilkis. While he turned towards her, the major was listening for Siraj's reply.

"I am his sister," Bilkis replied.

The major looked her up and down and echoed, "*Behn*?"

"Yes."

The major jerked his head towards Siraj and said, "Your brother?"

"Yes."

"Own brother?"

"Yes."

The major stared at one and then the other several times before saying, "There's a significant difference in age. Are there other siblings in between? Your parents must have given birth to some more traitors. Didn't they?"

They did not answer.

"Fine, you don't have to answer. I am aware that Bengalis breed like pigs and give birth to traitors. But even traitors can look decent." The major rose to his feet and walked up to Bilkis. After a while, he circled them slowly and returned to his position.

"You went to the marketplace."

His words met with silence.

"To remove the bodies? Didn't you know of the order?"

Silence again.

"You wanted to bury them? Who buried some bodies last night? Was it you?"

Both of them started. The major circled only Bilkis this time and came to stand before her.

"The grave was dug up by animals."

Bilkis felt her insides tightening.

"Don't you know that dogs don't need a burial?" The major screamed suddenly. He gave a sharp prod to Siraj on his stomach with his cane and made him move closer to Bilkis. Then he returned to his seat and continued to observe them with curiosity.

13

We will perform the last rites for the dead.

Like a two-storied structure without a support, like fragmented clouds or pieces of a landscape, like forms or movement lacking symmetry, the present is located in the here and now yet stretches into the unseen future. Human beings keep no stock of their inner reserves of strength. The innocence they try to cultivate is as fragile as glass, though only the hardest piece of diamond can cut it. When that happens the shards of innocence dissolve into oblivion because there can be no life without focusing on the here and now.

In truth reaction develops only in the presence of aggression and exists in the same way as a beautiful dream exists only in the context of a horror-filled reality or a sunny tomorrow is visualized only against the backdrop of a terrible nightmare; in the presence of profound crisis man necessarily has to seek refuge in imagining the opposite of the situation, his role becoming that of an athlete who stands before his own reflection in the mirror and attempts to twist two ends of a bar of iron and bring them together. He receives neither applause nor rest once the Herculean labor is over, because soon he is handed a second bar of unmalleable iron to work with.

It is I who made the earth and created man upon it. Man has no roots other than those that arise from the earth and though he can never return to her bosom, his deepest dialogue is with the earth and his utterances, by turn joyful or sad, of fusion or separation, derive from his attraction for the earth. That is why over time even the mother forgets the grief of losing her child or even a Ulysses rejects the prospect of immortality to return to the barren shores of his Ithaca.

We will return the dead to the same earth whence they sprang from, kneel down and cover their bodies with clods and return, without performing any ablution, buried under layers of the same earth, through the beleaguered reality of the present towards our cities, because is there anything more valuable than the wealth of our memories? Our cities that are now overrun with creepers and thorny bushes, our crops that are prematurely dead, our trees which bear rotten fruits, our wells which run dry, our roads where fierce creatures roam free while human beings hide in the woods. Our days which stir our fears and our nights which calm them. The wind now bears not the fragrance of flower but the stench that emanates from dead flesh in charnel houses. Yet our memories are not yet spoiled or erased, our wombs not yet barren, our manhood still not futile, our books not yet burnt, our potential not yet diminished. That is why man returns to his ravaged towns and cities to plant the seeds of memory anew. That is why Bilkis, too, stands silent.

Bilkis and Siraj were separated and taken to two different cells for questioning.

"Your name?"

"Siraj."

"Where are you from?"

"Jaleswari."

"Your sister's name?"

"Bilkis."

"Your religion?"

Though Bilkis was mentioned just before this question, the answer was still a lie difficult to take refuge in.

"Muslim."

"When did you go to India?"

"Never."

"When did you come back?"

"I've been here all along."

"How many have come from India?"

"No idea."

"What are their names? Where are they hiding?"

"I don't know."

"Who mined the bridge across the canal?"

"I don't know."

"Then what do you know?"

Silence.

"Can you recite the *kalma*?"

Silence.

"Do you know how to perform the namaz?"

Silence.

The major slapped Siraj's face hard and shouted, "Do you know how to fuck your sister?"

Siraj stood stunned. The major, who was secretly being assailed by lust at the thought of Bilkis's body and the possibility of enjoying her, seemed to derive some solace from hitting Siraj. He ordered the sentry sharply to carry on with the punishment and walked across to the room where Bilkis had been kept and from where Siraj's cries were clearly audible.

The moment he entered Bilkis glanced at the major.

The major came forward and said, "I am not going to punish you. Nor am I going to wring a confession out of you. Your brother will confess, sooner or later."

Silence.

"I am not going to force you, not even to give up your body to me."

Bilkis turned to the major and saw him smiling.

"You are going to come to me of your own volition."

Bilkis turned her face away. Siraj's cries in the next room turned to sobs and groans and then stopped.

Outside, day turned into night and the moon reappeared. The frame of the goalpost in the school playground looked like gallows from a distance. Bats hung from the eaves of the tin roof, a gecko could be heard in the distance. The major went out, returning after some time.

"Yes, you are going to come to me of your own free will. I won't force you. I never force anybody." The major could not help being reminded of a physical deficiency he possessed, that of ejaculating prematurely during intercourse. He tried to cover up for the deficiency, which simultaneously attracted him to women and made him despise them, by exaggerating his own importance.

"The truth is, I am an extremely compassionate man."

Silence.

"You have seen proof of that in my patience. My compatriots have forced many women into submission. I haven't."

Silence again.

"You will join me of your own free will. We've provided you with water, why haven't you taken a bath?"

Silence.

"We've brought you food. Why haven't you eaten?"

No reply.

"How far have you studied? You look educated. Do you speak English?"

Silence.

"I like women who can speak English. I believe such women understand the needs of a man's mind and of the different parts of his body."

Silence.

"Are you married? Of course you are. You look married. Does your husband, er, take you the same way each night?"

Silence.

"Where's your husband? Has he gone to India? Funny, isn't it? Whenever we execute somebody we tell his kith and kin when they make inquiries that so-and-so has gone away to India."

Silence.

"Answer me, does your husband make love to you the same way each night or in different ways?"

Receiving no answer, the major poured whiskey from a flask into a tumbler and drank slowly, his eyes never leaving Bilkis for a moment. Outside, the footsteps of sentries marching up and down could be heard.

"At least answer this one. Do you find me attractive?"

Silence.

"I can wait you know. I'm not on duty tonight and if I get a favorable reply, I can even keep myself free tomorrow night. Answer me in English if you don't know Urdu. I like women who speak English, I told you. Do you like me?" The major pulled up a chair and drew near.

"I can assure you that you are going to like me." The major poured himself another drink. "There's no reason why you wouldn't. My blood is pure and my seed of high quality. I can surely please a woman who takes the right initiative with me. Do I attract you? I will give you healthy children. A high quality harvest from high quality seed. Don't you want your offspring to be true, God-fearing Muslims, loyal Pakistanis at heart? We will give you such children . . . not just you but your sister, your mother . . . children who aren't born Hindu, who aren't traitors or unruly, who don't revolt, chant slogans or turn into communists. This is the service we are going to do for our race. We will purify your blood, implant true Pakistanis in your wombs and fly the flag of Islam high. You will be grateful for this, you will wait upon us and sing us songs with your melodious voices. I have heard that Bengalis can sing. Tell me once again, do I attract you?"

The major took a big swig of his drink and gazed at Bilkis with a satisfied look. There was no response from her; she kept staring at the wall.

The major lost his cool, threw his glass against the wall and screamed, "I told you that I am not going to force you. But I'll be damned if I am not going to watch a dog mount a bitch!"

Driven by a strong urge to undress Bilkis with his own hands, the major took a drunken step forward but could not summon up the necessary courage. He resisted the impulse to shoot her and put an end to the matter. Instead, he called his orderly and instructed him to strip her.

The orderly came forward and brusquely ordered Bilkis to get up. When Bilkis refused to stir, the orderly grabbed her arm and pulled.

"For heaven's sake, be more gentle," the major muttered irritably. Secretly he envied the powerful physique of the orderly and drank some more to stop thinking of it.

The habit of wearing clothes is ingrained in the human body through centuries of custom, and clothes constitute nothing short of a second layer of skin. Hence Bilkis was forced to react when she found this layer being unceremoniously pulled off her body. But her struggles were in vain and the orderly managed to take her sari off.

"Oh, ho! Patience, Jumma Khan, patience!" The major bellowed, thrashing about in his chair with suppressed arousal and rubbing his hands constantly, imagining the feel of Bilkis's body in the orderly's rough hands. When his eyes fell on her naked form, he looked away instinctively, shut his eyes, and rubbed his hands even harder, as if to shut out the memory of her nakedness. With his face still averted, he called the orderly and whispered an order to bring Siraj over.

Once the orderly left the room the major slowly turned his head towards Bilkis, blinked at her shyly at first and then opened his eyes wide to take in the sight of her nude form. He stood up on his feet and whispered to himself, "*What a beautiful body*!"

Siraj was brought into the room by the sentry with the short, stout gun, whose face remained expressionless even at the sight that met his eyes. Standing at the door he stared in a disciplined fashion at the doorframe. Siraj, however, closed his eyes the moment they fell on Bilkis and stood looking beaten and haggard. Bilkis did not close hers but continued to look in front of her with a steady gaze.

The major circled Siraj once and then barked at the orderly, "Strip this one too."

Siraj opened his eyes in shock, but the moment he saw Bilkis again he shut them, wrapping his arms around his own waist.

The orderly tried to prise his shirt off him and, failing, simply tore it off. Siraj immediately fell on his knees, and with his arms still around his waist curled his body into a fetal position. His whole frame shook with uncontrollable spasms.

With a sharp kick, the major knocked Siraj to the floor. The orderly pounced on him immediately, straddling his chest with his knees and trying to tear his fly open.

"No!" Siraj screamed.

Bilkis stood still, holding her breath and her body, too, racked by shivers she could not control.

"No-o-o!"

The major placed a heavy boot on Siraj's chest and roared, "Bengalis are nothing but dogs! Dogs have no sisters!"

The orderly managed to force Siraj's arms open and placed one knee on each of them to pin them down. Then he got to work on his fly again.

"No! No! No!"

The orderly rapidly unbuttoned the fly. Bilkis shut her eyes and her body grew still.

The orderly stared before him at first with an uncomprehending look, stumped by what he saw. The next moment he jumped to his feet and yelled with excitement: "Sir, *yeh toh Hindu hai*! This one's a Hindu!"

14

Bilkis picked up the sari lying at her feet and put it on, doing away with the niceties of draping it properly, and merely ensured that her modesty was adequately covered.

A captain and a few soldiers had rushed in. The major now silently asked them to leave.

"Can we be of any service, Sir?" The captain asked. The major shook his head. The captain and other soldiers departed and only the guard who had brought Pradip in was left. Once again the major silently ordered him to move the body away. But the moment the guard bent down to pull it away Bilkis spoke, for the very first time, a brief, sharp "No" which echoed in the room.

The major was taken aback by the determination behind that "No." Thinking it over briefly, he ordered the guard to leave the room. After standing immobile for some time he returned to his chair and slumped into it exhausted. "I don't like dead bodies," he said. "They remind me of defeat."

Bilkis walked slowly up to Pradip's body lying on the floor and knelt down next to it in the same, deliberate fashion. She kept staring at the dark red blood oozing from it, blood that appeared almost artificial in the light of the Petromax lamp. The major searched for his glass and remembered having smashed it some time back. He drank straight from the flask, his face puckered in an expression of regret, whether for the glass or Pradip, one could not make out.

"What will you do with him now?" Bilkis asked, her eyes still on Pradip.

Evading the answer, the major simply said, "Why did he try to take the sentry's gun? He lost his life."

Silence.

"Though he would have died anyway." The major continued. "We would have sent him off to India after securing his confession." He smiled briefly at his own joke.

"Will you leave him lying here?"

The major continued to smile.

"Like the bodies of the others in the market?"

The major gulped the last drops from the flask and stretched his legs. "Look at me," he commanded her.

Bilkis closed Pradip's open eyes with her own hand.

"You know, I have never seen a Hindu woman naked." The major seemed to have digested the story of Bilkis and Pradip being siblings and taken Bilkis for a Hindu.

Bilkis put her hand on Pradip's cheek.

"Tell me, do Hindus bathe every day?"

Silence.

"Is it true that Hindu women stink?"

Silence.

"Do they keep their private parts clean?"

Silence.

"I am told that the Hindu cunt resembles a bitch's. It's difficult to extricate oneself from it once the job is done. Is it true?"

Silence.

"How long do you think you'll be able to hold me inside you?"

Bilkis moved her eyes off Pradip and looked directly at the major. "I want to perform his last rites," she said.

"I am now in a mood to force you, you know."

Bilkis came and stood before the major, who moved his leg back instinctively. "Take off that sari," he muttered, his jowls tightening and a vein beginning to throb on his temple.

"First, I want to hold my brother's funeral." Bilkis spoke softly.

The major's jowls slackened, the throbbing vein disappeared and his eyes looked pleased. He got up and placed a hand on her shoulder. Bilkis moved away.

"All right. I told you I can be patient. We'll bury him. It won't take long to dig a grave in the school playground."

"No."

"What, then?"

"He won't be buried."

The major gave a whistle. "Oh, I forgot that he's a Hindu. Hindus burn their bodies. Why, I wonder."

Silence.

"Maybe because the Lord fashioned men from the earth and Satan from fire. That's why Hindus go back to the fire once they die."

Silence.

"Fire." The major uttered the word deliberately, dwelling on it. "A couple of tins of petrol should be enough. What do you think?"

"No."

"That's enough to burn a body."

"I'll need wood. Preferably sandalwood."

"Sandalwood?" The major whistled again and shrugged in amusement. Bilkis felt the steady resolve of the night before returning to her silently.

"Plain wood will do."

"Where do I get wood at this hour of the night?"

"I don't know."

"Are you testing my patience?"

Silence.

"In that case let's wait till daybreak. I'll have the Biharis make arrangements for your brother's funeral. I am ready to wait. You?" His smile widened, indicating that he meant he was ready to wait for Bilkis. When Bilkis replied that she too was ready, the major was not perturbed, though her words had been uttered in an entirely different context. What the major did not know was that she had braced herself for what was to come from the moment she closed Pradip's eyes and felt his cheeks. He could not make out that her brief reply had been given in an even, detached tone, dissociated from the present.

"I want him cremated by the bank of the river. Not here."

"Why by the bank of the river?" The major threw Bilkis a sharp look, the haze induced by alcohol and lust lifting momentarily off his mind. He wondered if this was a ploy. The Indian border was not far from the other side of the river, barely thirty miles as the crow flies.

"Hindus cremate their dead by the river."

"Strange." The major shrugged again. "Fine, I'll check with the Biharis. If they confirm that Hindus cremate their dead by the river, we'll do the same. Tell me something—didn't one of your goddesses have five husbands?"

"Yes."

The major gave a long whistle.

The day dawned and found Bilkis seated next to Pradip's body, motionless like a figure carved out of stone. She sat there for a long time, trying now and then to wipe the blood off his body with the edge of her sari. Some of it could be removed, but several large stains remained, creating a pattern like an archipelago on a map.

The major returned at midday. "Come." He told her.

Four or five Bihari boys, possibly the ones who had discovered and captured them in the market, carried Pradip's body out to a pickup truck. The major told Bilkis to board the back of the truck and went up to sit in front with the driver. A couple of soldiers also jumped into the back as the truck roared off. The truck crossed the school playground and went down the deserted streets of Jaleswari in the blinding sunlight in the direction of the Adhkosha, the roar of its engine sounding incongruous in the silence pervading all around.

A few more Bihari youth waited near the riverbank, guarding a pile of wood. The river bank lay deserted. The water was still and not a bird was in sight. Bilkis got off the truck when it reached its destination and walked barefoot over the sandy bank, barely feeling its heat. The major too got off the truck and stood next to it with his legs planted wide apart. The Biharis waited for his orders, speaking softly among themselves, throwing him inquiring looks from time to time and casting respectful looks at the armed soldiers accompanying him.

Though Bilkis had never witnessed a cremation, let alone arrange one, she managed to assemble the pile of wood into the semblance of a pyre from some unconscious blueprint within herself. Remembering the way wood was placed in a hearth, she lined up two rows of wood so that the flames could spread evenly and fast. Then she cast a look at the major who silently ordered the Biharis to remove Pradip's body from the back of the truck. They carried the body to the makeshift pyre and quietly waited for instructions from Bilkis. Receiving a silent but clear signal from her, they placed the body on the pyre and quickly moved away to gather around the van.

Bilkis took one look at Pradip's face, glistening in the sun and looked away. She covered his body with more wood and stood still near his head. The picture of Khoka's body lying in the market rose before her eyes momentarily, like a faraway vision.

The major, who had been watching her activities from afar, now walked down the sandy slope followed by a soldier carrying a tin of petrol to speed up the proceedings. The major was not sure how long the pile of wood would take to catch fire otherwise. The soldier doused the pyre with petrol and went away. Bilkis noted the movements around her dimly, her mind fixed on the funeral she was about to officiate at. Soon, the body lying before her lost all semblance of a human form and appeared to be a vision of Death itself, lying before her.

Ordered by the major, a Bihari youth threw her a matchbox. When she set fire to the pile of wood both the dead and Death vanished into the flames which leaped up before her eyes. Bilkis stared into the conflagration, unable to take her eyes off it.

The major ordered two Bihari boys to escort her back. But when they pulled at her arms, Bilkis refused to move. They pulled, harder this time.

"Gently, gently . . . " the major murmured, irritated by the sight of the boys feeling her soft, female body. After some time he walked further down the slope and stood next to her. The boys stepped back, looking confused. "What's troubling you now?" The major asked Bilkis.

Bilkis remained silent. Behind her, sudden ripples appeared in the river.

The smell of burning flesh assailed the major's senses and in spite of being a soldier he found it difficult not to feel nauseous. He raised a hand to his face to ward off the great heat generated by the burning fire. With the other hand, he tried to drag Bilkis away.

It was at that moment that Bilkis turned and clasped his body in a tight embrace. The major was at first taken aback and then panicked when he realized that the woman was pressing him against the burning pyre with superhuman might. With terrified eyes he saw her hair and clothes catch fire and felt an excruciating agony in his own back as it burned. He tried to push her off his body and jump away but the woman seemed made of fire itself and impossible to dislodge. The fleeting thought crossed his mind that while man was made of earth, Satan was made of flames. Possessed by atavistic terror, his body trembled one last time.

Her own body now turned into an incandescent firebrand, Bilkis continued to press his body against the pyre.